WHAT OTHERS ARE SAYING

Sometimes when you read the stories behind a man it can be a shock and disappointment learning what influenced a person. In this case, you are laughing so hard the tears will stain your book. Tannenbaum gives a very candid and humorous backstory to his early days with the law. Written in such a way that you can devour it in one sitting or chapter-by-chapter and it does not disappoint.

Griff Mangan ~ Paragraphs On Padre *Book Store*

I loved, loved, loved *Adventures in the Law* by David Harry Tannenbaum. This is a first-rate and entertaining adventure in reading and I was enthralled by the humorous yet inclusive cases Tannenbaum has tackled over the decades in which he practiced law. Tannenbaum recounts 27 tales in a *Reader's Digest* short story fashion in which each character takes on a permanent life of his/her own, from Zuro, the irascible Greek, to the author's very own mother who judges clients as good or bad by her keen intuition alone. This book can easily be compared with Dr. Oliver Sachs' quirky case studies of his patients in his memorable book, *The Man Who Mistook His Wife for a Hat.*

Prepare yourself for a roller coaster ride of weird stories and surprise endings. Let me assure you, you will love *Adventures in the Law* by David Harry Tannenbaum. It is an entertaining and compelling follow-up to his well-known *Padre Island Mysteries.*

Richard Conrath ~ *Author* Cooper's Moon

ADVENTURES IN THE LAW

WEIRD AND FUNNY TALES TOLD BY THE LAWYER WHO LIVED THEM

DAVID HARRY TANNENBAUM

Red Engine Press
Pittsburgh, Pennsylvania

LIBRARY OF CONGRESS CONTROL NUMBER: 2018906754

ISBN: 978-0-9963650-1-7 TRADE PAPERBACK
ISBN: 978-0-9963650-2-4 EBOOK

PRINTED IN THE UNITED STATES.

RED ENGINE PRESS
HOT RAY IMPRINT
PITTSBURGH, PA

CONFESSIONS

Confession One

I was a lawyer for almost fifty years before retiring from that noble profession. I was, specifically, an intellectual property lawyer (think "patents"), with no speaking parts in court.

Confession Two

Well, Confession One is not exactly accurate. I routinely performed pro bono work—assigned by a judge to represent people who found themselves on the wrong side of the law and without sufficient means to pay for a lawyer of their choice. In that role, I did defend some folks accused of criminal behavior. And, of course, I did speak in court when the judge allowed me to do so, often not very eloquently, as you will observe from the adventures reported herein.

Confession Three

I also maintained a very small general law (not to be confused with intellectual property law) practice early in my legal career, representing clients who could not afford lawyers with fancy offices.

Confession Four

Legal ethics and privacy being what they are, the names, locations, and time frames have all been changed.

Confession Five

I'm a fiction writer at heart, so be warned that not all the facts I relate are one hundred percent accurate. Some would call this literary license, which is a polite way of saying that I've fictionalized the dialog. I have convinced myself that the obfuscations serve to better protect the characters while preserving the true nature of their machinations. But the truth is that I am unable to depict myself as being as slow-witted as I felt in most of these situations. So for the most part, the fiction is mostly designed to make my performance appear better than it actually was.

DEDICATION

Writers dedicate books to their spouses, children, friends, teachers, you name it. I initially thought that I would dedicate this book to the clients and others who appear in these stories, but I have taken enough license with the facts that I doubt they would recognize themselves. So, instead I hereby dedicate this book to ALL of you who, over my nearly fifty years in the law, have allowed me to handle your legal needs. I remain privileged to have been a part of your life and, I hope, to have helped where I could.

TALES

FIRE IN THE
HOLE

(Where There's Smoke...)

In my book *THE PADRE PARANOIA* (written under the pen name of David Harry) published in 2012, I wrote the following:

In Memoriam

I want to publicly acknowledge Professor Emeritus John Sullivan for his many years of teaching law at Capital Law School in Columbus, Ohio. I am forever grateful to him for his dedication to teaching and to the energy he brought to the classroom. He not only taught me, but also changed my life in the process. He may be gone, but he is certainly not forgotten.

Professor Sullivan is certainly not forgotten. I couldn't write a book involving the law without thinking of him. He was short, but yet a giant of a man, in voice alone if not in height. Each class with John Sullivan lasted three hours, with a ten-minute break beginning at ten to the hour. While the door wasn't actually locked (I think only because of fire safety codes), woe be unto any person who opened the door during the fifty minutes of class time. It just didn't happen. Being on time meant being in your seat, ready to discuss the assigned cases, at least two minutes before the hour. Being unprepared also was not an option. If your name was called, you stood. And you remained standing, fielding his barrage of questions until he exhausted your knowledge of the subject. He had a way of changing the facts ever so slightly with each question until you found yourself coming around from the other end. What if the victim was standing still? What if he was moving away from the perpetrator? What if he was coming toward the perpetrator? What if he reached toward his pocket? What if there was bad blood between them? What if the perpetrator was the victim's former husband? What if...What if...What if...? Nuance after nuance after nuance, the questions from Professor Sullivan continued to flood in until it became second nature to see the facts not only for what they seemed to be, but also for what they might be.

Just when you thought you were done, there was always more. "Okay now, Tannenbaum," he might bellow, "what if Count Bamoonatoon thought the gun was unloaded and pulled the trigger in jest?" (Bamoonatoon was his go-to hypothetical character, always in trouble, as often as not the result of his untimely presence at his favorite bar, The Upholstered Sewer.) "Argue the case from that perspective. Go!"

Any student coming to class without anxiety was in for a rude awakening. In fact, most of those who seemed the most self-assured fell victim to the school's high attrition rate and were notably absent when we reconvened for the second year of class.

Near the end of one semester, I walked into Professor Sullivan's class six minutes early because the traffic had been light. There he was, an uncharacteristic smile on his face, standing behind a big box of cigars. "It's a girl!" the pink band proclaimed.

"Who had the baby?" I asked as I reached for a cigar, thinking that it was the dean, or possibly another professor.

"What's the matter, Tannenbaum? Don't you think I have what it takes to father a baby?"

"Oh, no...no, Professor. Only...only, that you haven't said anything about your wife being pregnant." In all honesty, I didn't even know he had a wife. At least I had the good sense to keep that tidbit to myself.

"I didn't know myself."

How that could be I couldn't imagine. And I wasn't brave enough to ask.

"You look like you don't believe me."

"I...I..."

"Doctors thought it was a tumor. She went in yesterday to have it removed and some young intern did something he was not supposed to do. He gave her an X-ray, and there was the baby."

The story made no sense to me, but I had no intention of debating John Sullivan. The room was already filling with smoke as the students lit up their cigars in a building that had "no smoking" signs posted every fifty feet. I found a seat next to a window so I'd be out of the mainstream of the smoke. This promised to be an interesting three hours, but I had no inkling of just how interesting it would prove to be.

The smoke stayed in the center of the room for the first hour or so, sparing my lungs for the most part. Sullivan called my name twice with questions designed to challenge anything I answered. I think he was singling me out because, sitting where I was, I might have been the only student he could see clearly. Or maybe it was because I had questioned his fathering capabilities. With Professor Sullivan, one never knew.

About halfway through the second hour, I glanced out of the window and saw that the alley three floors below was filled with flashing lights. I leaned even closer to the window to get a better look at what was going on down there.

"Tannenbaum!" Sullivan shouted, "Pay attention! From your performance here tonight you should be the last one to let your attention wander."

"But...but I think..."

"Frankly, I don't give a ragged hoot what you think. Pay attention or get out!"

The flashing lights down below got stronger, and I could hear more sirens arriving by the minute.

"Tannenbaum!"

I stood. "Yes, sir," I replied.

"Are you paying attention?"

"There are fire trucks in the alley."

"And you've never seen a fire truck before? Of what relevance to my class is this exciting fact?"

"But..."

"If your goal is to be a lawyer, turn to face me! If you'd like to be a fireman instead, then go out there and join them! I'm sure they could use your help. But you can't do both! So what's it going to be? We're all waiting to hear your decision."

"Lawyer, sir."

"Then turn and face me. And if I see you looking out that window one more time that's where you'll be the rest of the year! Out in the alley!"

Before I could answer, a loud knock on the classroom door caused all eyes to swivel away from me.

"Go away!" Sullivan bellowed. "At least some of us are learning the law in here!"

When we opened the door five minutes later to take our break, two firemen, axes in hand, rushed in and began chopping a hole in the middle of the wooden classroom floor. Then a third fireman appeared with a fire extinguisher and flushed the hole with foam. Apparently, one of the students had pushed his still burning cigar into a hole in the floor that had accumulated paper and other debris over the years. The fire had spread under the floor and had taken down the ceiling below.

When the ten-minute break was over, Sullivan demanded that the firemen leave.

"It could reignite," one of them said. "We didn't know anyone was up here, or we would have..."

"If it's out, it's out!" Sullivan bellowed. "Break time's over! We'll keep an eye on it. Now go, we have another hour and you, dear fellow, are wasting it. Now out! And keep the racket down!"

The firemen left. The door was closed. And class resumed. Sullivan had repositioned me away from the window and I was now sitting in the center of the class directly behind the hole. "Tannenbaum wants to be a fireman," he told the class. "It seems he likes the flashing lights and the red trucks more than he likes the law. Keep guard over that hole and keep us safe for an hour, won't you Tannenbaum?"

"Yes, sir." I slid lower in my chair, half hoping to disappear into that very ash-laden hole.

When the hour was up, we marched out the door and down the steps, only to find the entire building, indeed the entire block, had been evacuated. Only our class had continued uninterrupted, because no one in the school administration had had the courage to tell Professor Sullivan to end his class early. The building had filled with smoke, but given all the smoke from Sullivan's celebratory cigars, we were none the wiser.

A takeaway from my time with John Sullivan, with whom I had several more courses over the next few years, is how easily "Yes, Your Honor" flowed from my lips when a judge lectured me in open court.

Another takeaway is how many years it took me before I could sit through a law-themed movie. It was a full seven years after law school that my wife and I went to see the movie The Paper Chase. A law professor, played by John Houseman, was grilling the class on some subject or another.

My wife nudged me. "David," she said. "We have to leave."

I thought she was having a problem, so I followed her out of the theater. "What's the problem?" I asked. "Something wrong with you?"

"It's you! If we had stayed any longer, I think you'd have had a heart attack."

"I...I just felt I was back with John Sullivan and unprepared for his class. Like I hadn't read all the cases, and the names were not coming fast enough. How did you know?"

"You were slouching in your seat, mumbling and twisting around and scratching your head wildly!"

"I wanted to see that movie."

"Maybe ten years from now. Maybe never. We're going home."

* * *

I saw John Sullivan exactly three times after I walked across the stage in the purple regalia of a newly minted Juris Doctor.

The first time was when my family and I were driving through Columbus, Ohio and on a lark I suggested we stop and visit the new law school building.

"Are you thinking what I think you're thinking?" my wife asked once we were inside. "If it has to do with John Sullivan, it would be nice to stop in and say hello."

"You know me all too well," I answered.

"It's been, what, twenty years since you graduated? How many students has he had in that time? You expect him to remember you?"

"Probably, not," I replied, actually glad she had spared me the humiliation of the blank stare I was sure to receive from my old teacher.

"But there's certainly no harm in trying," she continued. "The kids might get a kick out of meeting the man you always talk about."

No backing out now, I realized.

We found the professor's office but, to my relief, the door was closed. "I'll just send him a note," I said, turning away.

Just then a law school classmate of mine, now a professor at the school, happened by. "David!" she exclaimed. "What brings you to Columbus?"

"Just driving through. Thought I'd stop and check out the new building."

"Did you see John Sullivan?"

"His door's closed. I'll send him a note."

"Don't be silly. Just knock. He's with a student."

So knock I did. And then took a step back, half expecting the door to blow open in my face, which it almost did.

"Who's making that racket!" bellowed a voice through the door, a voice that instantly brought back all-too-vivid memories of not being able to answer Professor Sullivan's questions in class. "Don't just make noise. Open the door and come in!"

Sucking in the air as if it would be my last breath, I forced my hand to turn the knob.

"Tannenbaum!" Professor Sullivan exclaimed as I timidly pushed open the door. "How the hell are you?" He turned to the student across his desk. "You!" he shouted. "Get out and come back later! I have some catching up to do!

"Come on in and sit down, Tannenbaum, and tell me what the hell you've made of yourself. What's it been, nineteen years?"

"Yes, sir. Nineteen." What's this guy have, a yearbook in his head?

How he remembered me I'll never know. I must have done something right—or perhaps just the opposite.

The second time I saw John Sullivan was at a class reunion, and the last time was over breakfast in a diner after he had retired. His mind was as sharp as ever and he spoke of the law with the same passion as he had fifty years earlier when I sat—or should I say, quivered—in his class as a first-year.

Perhaps the knots in my stomach weren't as tight that morning, but they were there just the same.

ZURO

(My Favorite Greek)

The ink on my law degree was still damp, and the license from the Ohio State Bar hadn't yet come back from the frame shop, when Zuro came into my legal life

It all began when a friend and fellow law school graduate just launching his career asked me to help him with a case. My friend, Butch, had a client trying to collect two thousand dollars owed to him by a man named Zuro. The client had tried every which way to get Zuro to repay the loan, all to no avail. Butch was about to start a job with the state, but agreed to take the case, figuring he could make a quick few bucks before the job actually started.

Well, no.

Zuro was a pro at dodging collection agents and the like. It wasn't as if he was broke. In fact, just the opposite. Zuro owned rental properties and several businesses, including, as I later found out, a very profitable diner. He just disliked having to repay his debts.

Zuro had actually signed a promissory note for the two-thousand-dollar loan, and I asked myself how difficult could it be to collect a debt that is acknowledged in writing? What I had no clue about was the effort it takes to collect from a professional deadbeat.

Butch had actually filed suit against Zuro, but had been unable to have him served with the court papers. Zuro was a master at dodging process servers as well as collection lawyers and could never be found at any of his known places of business. So my first problem was to figure out how to find a man who never appeared at any business he owned and who had no publicly available home address. (As I later found out, Zuro was present at his various businesses, but under a different name, and his employees, if they knew his true identity, kept it to themselves.)

As it turned out, our client—the man to whom Zuro owed the two thousand—somehow knew that Zuro picked up his dry cleaning at the Apollo Laundry around 9 a.m. every Wednesday. So I hired a process server to lie in wait for Mr. Zuro, whom I had dubbed "The Phantom," to fetch his freshly laundered shirts on the following Wednesday. Just as predicted, a black Lincoln Town Car pulled up in front of the Apollo Laundry at 9:05 Wednesday morning, and out stepped an immaculately dressed large man. I took a picture of his license plate while the process server followed him inside and served him.

The license plate led me to an address to which I sent a set of interrogatories, which are a series of questions that a defendant, like Zuro, must answer within a given time period. Many of the questions dealt with Zuro's bank accounts. Where were they located? Who had control over them? The amounts in each? Names and addresses of all his businesses, that type of thing, mostly designed to encourage a defendant to give up and pay up.

It worked!

A two-thousand dollar check arrived in my mail four days later. My fee, after expenses, was $100.

"Did you receive my check?" Zuro asked when I answered my phone a few days later.

"I did. And my client thanks you," I replied, uncomfortable as to where this was going.

"Please come to my home tomorrow night at seven. I have some business to discuss with you."

"I can't represent you if that is what you are asking."

"It is. And why not? Our little matter is finished. The suit has been dropped, and unless you have other matters against me I believe you are free to represent me."

Zuro had a point. The conflict was gone.

Before I could answer, Zuro added, "You will be well compensated for your time. That much I can assure you."

What could be the harm of meeting with him? So I dutifully arrived at precisely seven o'clock. Only thing was, I was across the street from where the Lincoln Town Car was parked.

I rang the doorbell and waited.

No answer.

"Over here!" A big voice boomed from behind me. "That's my brother's house. We're all over here." (It turns out that Zuro's Lincoln was registered at his brother's address.)

I walked slowly across the street; second-, third- and fourth-guessing the wisdom of my being there. With every step I took, the urge to run and hide increased. But lawyers don't run and hide. Or do they? I had witnessed politicians making themselves scarce when they were on the wrong side of an issue. Okay, David, make up an excuse and hightail it over to your car. There is still time.

Time ran out when the big man extended his hand in a gesture of friendship. Like a seasoned politician, I extended mine in return.

Wrong move for a guy whose plan was to run and hide. He pulled me to him and embraced me as if we were long lost family. Old country custom, I figured, but I was now a captive of this bear-like man.

"Come in! Come in! Welcome to my home. We will break bread together. I hope you're hungry. My wife has prepared a traditional Greek dinner. My brother will be joining us."

This was a home visit, so for me no tie. Wrong! Zuro was wearing a jacket and tie. I entered, only to discover another giant and two semi-giants in the living room, all similarly attired. But what really caught my attention was the large table in the adjoining dining room with place settings all around. It wasn't that I disliked Greek food. Just the opposite. But the truth was that I had just completed a rather large dinner at home.

Zuro introduced me around. The two semi-giants were his sons and the other giant his brother. Dozens of children, or so it seemed (actual count, six) scampered around. Then the women appeared. Two daughters-in-law, a sister-in-law, and finally my host's wife. A tall woman with bright green eyes. Cat's eyes. Very active and friendly cat's eyes.

"You will be joining us for dinner, I understand," the wife said, a hint of a Greek accent dancing around the edges of her words.

"I just..."

"Of course, Mr. T will be joining us," Zuro announced. "He's the new family lawyer, and it would not be proper to exclude him from our meal. I hope you enjoy Greek cooking, Mr. T, because Helena is the best. It's her recipes that we use at the diner."

What diner? I asked myself. And I'm not the family lawyer! Better stop this before it becomes a runaway train. But the train had already become a runaway, and I didn't know where to find the big red panic stop button. Either I misread the curriculum, or that wasn't a subject taught in my law school.

For all I can remember, it was perhaps the best Greek food I have ever eaten, but all I can recall these many years later is the pain of an over-extended stomach and me forcing more and more food down my gullet while not allowing any of the previous forkfuls to escape.

And that was before dessert was brought out.

It was after ten, and the two sons and their families had gone. It was just Zuro, his brother and me in the living room, the three us with huge cigars hanging from our lips (although their cigars didn't seem so huge in proportion to their faces). "Here," Zuro said, "these files are for you."

I had to clear the smoke from my eyes to see what Zuro was pointing at. "These all appear to be collection matters," I said. "That's not..."

"One is litigation. A building we contracted for and the seller backed out. Sold it for a million more than our deal. Nice piece of change for you. Get us our money and you get one-third."

"Speaking of fees, what..."

"Thirty-three percent. That's what you get for all of these. Collections, contracts whatever. A full third."

And point three-three, the engineer side of my brain whimpered. "Plus out-of-pocket expenses," I added, not bringing up the missing decimal that would make Zuro's thirty-three percent equal a "full third." Actually, hearing the million-dollar number caused me to assume a million dollar judgment, and my mind had focused on that profit number. I had begun spending my already-earned $333,333.33.

"Fine, but run those expenses by us before you spend our money."

"Why me?" I asked. "I have no practice yet. No office. You know I'm just out of law school. Surely..."

"Hungry. You have nothing else, so you can spend time getting us our money. And...and frankly, you're the first lawyer in town to collect anything from us. If you can do that, then you can get our money from these bums!" Zuro slapped the files for emphasis. "There's cases in here worth over a hundred big ones. Not counting the money you can get us for the building. Oughta keep you going for a long, long time."

He was right about that. The lure of the money certainly outweighed the stench of working for an admitted deadbeat. But what I didn't yet know was that Zuro's real plan was to recoup from me the two thousand he had paid to my client.

Later that night I sorted through the files with the intention of picking the easy ones to work on first. The ones that required an outlay of expense money, I decided to handle only after I had been paid for settling the easy ones. Put another way. I planned to advance the expenses out of house money.

The first matter was simple. Zuro was owed $120 for a bounced rent check. One phone call and the man mailed the check—directly to Zuro.

Zuro owed me thirty-nine dollars and sixty cents. Easy pickings. Or so it seemed at first.

Two other files were delinquent rent matters, and one entailed damage that exceeded the damage deposit. In each case, the debtor paid immediately, but in all three cases, they insisted on making the check payable to Zuro. Within two weeks, Zuro owed me two hundred eighty-seven dollars and twenty-nine cents.

I was on a roll. But the real big ones were breach of contract cases, each worth in the neighborhood of $50,000, and that's not counting the possible million-dollar case. I was gearing up.

I dug out a file that appeared to be worth $1,800, as best I could determine. Zuro's brother had delivered an oriental rug for dry cleaning and the cleaner had ruined the rug.

"Piece of shit! Pardon my French," the dry cleaner yelled across the counter when I stopped by his store to discuss the matter with him. "See that bastard in court, that's what I want."

"Run that one by me again," I responded, not knowing what the man was saying. I couldn't determine if he meant Zuro's brother was a piece of shit or the carpet?

"He delivered a rug, all right. I'll give him that. It was rolled up and tied. Said it was a family heirloom or something. When we unrolled it, there were holes everywhere. At first I thought moths. Then one of my employees noticed burn marks. The holes were made when someone tried to cut out the burn spots. Cigarette burns, the best we can make out. Bastard is running a scam. See you in court, counselor."

"Have any pictures?" I asked, trying to keep the conversation going.

"You want pictures, sue me. I'll show you pictures. Now get out before I throw you out!"

Truth be known, I believed the shop owner. That one wasn't going anywhere on my watch.

Next came a promissory note for six thousand dollars. "Sure, I signed it," confessed the man known to me only as Jimmy. "But too bad for you, it's a gambling debt. Illegal. Not enforceable. Nada. Nothing. Don't call again."

Dead phone.

Time to talk to Zuro.

ME: I assume you got the $1,600 I collected for you?

ZURO: What of it?

ME: My fee. Thirty-three percent as we agreed.

ZURO: Lawyers take theirs out first. I thought you did that.

ME: Check came straight to you.

ZURO: That's too bad. Next time take it first.

ME: Should I come over to your house or will you mail me a check?

The line went dead.

I threw his files in a box, saying, "Good riddance!" Only the language I used was a bit more graphic—and a lot more satisfying.

Skip forward several months. I accepted a corporate job in another state. While packing the house, I came upon Zuro's box of files.

Ethical dilemma. I had a lien on the files for the unpaid fee. However, the lien did not allow me to take the files out of state.

I called a lawyer friend and asked if I could store the box of files at his law firm. He was not to release the files—or even peek in the box—without my written permission.

He agreed.

I moved. I sent a letter to Zuro with my new address and phone number.

Two weeks later, my phone exploded with the sound of a very angry Zuro demanding, in extremely graphic language, the return of his files. Threats of disbarment rolled from the receiver for "removing his very valuable files from the state!"

When Zuro finally calmed down, it turned out one of the contract matters suddenly had taken on a new life, but he required the signed copy of the contract, which, of course, was in the box of files I had in my possession.

ME: You finished yelling?

ZURO: You ready for me to file a grievance with the Bar?

ME: The files are in your city, so stop your threats.

ZURO: You have no right to...

ME: You owe me money. I have a lien on the files. Pay me, you get the files. Simple.

ZURO: [Expletives deleted.]

ME: You done yet?

ZURO: Who has them?

ME: When your check clears, you get the location.

ZURO: I need that contract today!

ME: I needed that money three months ago!

ZURO: [More expletives deleted].

ME: Goodbye Mr. Zuro. You'll get the address when the check clears. You have my address.

Now it was my turn to hang up.

Three days later, the check arrived. I deposited it. I called the banker and asked him to let me know when the funds cleared.

Zuro called twice before the banker called me back and confirmed the deposit secure.

On Zuro's third call, I gave him the location of the files. I had already sent release information to my friend, since I expected Zuro to pick up the files immediately.

Which he did within an hour of my giving him the address.

I know that, because two hours after Zuro received the file location from me my friend called. "Wish I had known who your client was," he began, "cause I would have withheld those files. That (more expletives) owes our firm a ton of money, as he does every major law firm in town. No one will handle him any longer. To my knowledge, you're the only lawyer to collect legal fees from that S.O.B. Congratulations. He's one dangerous man. Be glad you're rid of him—and out of state."

And I was.

BILLY BOB

(Part One)

If Billy Bob Johnson had lived, he would have proclaimed me the greatest lawyer in the world. And, I suppose, from his limited perspective, he would have been correct.

But he didn't live. And, of course, I'm nothing of the sort. In fact, in the matters I handled for him, luck and happenstance played a far greater role than did any legal prowess I can claim credit for.

The saga began when I answered an ad in the newspaper for a free road atlas. Toll-free 800 numbers were relatively new at that point, and I ventured to call one. The voice recording instructed me to leave my name and address and then went on to say that "the package will be delivered within a month."

Little did I know that the delivery mechanism for the atlas would be a magazine salesman. A smooth-talking gentleman called, informed me that he had my atlas, and asked for the best time to hand-deliver it. Despite my telling him several times to simply leave it at the front door, he wore me down, all very politely, I might add. Tuesday nights, my wife went ice-skating, which meant I had the task of putting the children to bed. A task that was completed by eight. I suggested to my caller that he could deliver the atlas after 8 p.m. on the following Tuesday. Much to my surprise, he accepted.

Billy Bob arrived on my doorstep at the appointed time, atlas in hand. Upon learning my wife was absent, he said, "If there's one thing I've learned selling magazines, it's that it's impossible without the wife being present." He went on to complain that his leg was killing him and he needed to sit a while.

If there is one thing I've learned over the years, it's that if a con artist can't con you, then by definition he's not a con artist after all. Billy Bob was one of the best. So in he came, sat on my sofa, drank my water, and within a few minutes knew my life story.

"So write," he pronounced, "if that's what you enjoy. Write for fun. Be a lawyer by day and a writer by night. What's wrong with that plan?"

"Nothing," I confessed, more by way of dismissing the conversation than really embracing the plan.

"Hey, I like you. How about you representing me for the car accident?"

Instead of simply saying no thanks, that's not my area of the law, I said, "What accident?" Apparently I was still under the influence of his con.

Billy Bob proceeded to tell me how he had stepped out of his car in front of his apartment building and a speeding vehicle clipped the edge of his car door, causing the door to bounce back and slam into his leg. I started to consider that his limp was not the con I had thought it had been, and I felt foolish for thinking it had been. So much for my human compassion—and naïveté.

I explained to Billy Bob that I was not qualified to handle personal injury, but to no avail. He wrote out his address on a slip of paper and said he wanted a retainer agreement mailed to him as soon as I could. To encourage him to leave, I nodded okay.

I had no idea of how to even find such a retainer agreement. The Internet was still years in the future, and I was reduced to asking around. A colleague suggested a legal supply store, and the Yellow Pages came to my rescue. A few days later, I bought a pad of general purpose retainer forms, filled one out as best I could, and dropped it in the mail.

A week passed and, truth be told, I felt relieved, yet a bit peeved, that I hadn't heard back from Billy Bob. But then a woman by the name of Melody called, claiming to be Billy Bob's wife. She needed to see me, "as soon as humanly possible!" She found my name on the retainer agreement that had arrived at her house, and she needed a lawyer immediately. "If Billy Bob asked you to represent him, then you must be good. He's a great judge of people. And I need a good lawyer."

Picturing her smooth-talking husband sitting in my living room driving me crazy, all I could think of was divorce. "If this is a divorce matter, then I can't represent..."

"Heavens no! Not a divorce. I'd never divorce him. This is really important! Can I come to your home tonight? Same time as Billy Bob? Eight, wasn't it?"

Who was the better con artist, Mr. or Mrs.? I still can't say. But clearly they both had my number.

Melody arrived fifteen minutes early while I was out running an errand. My wife chatted with her and learned that Melody was newly pregnant, this being her second. This fact was not communicated to me at the time, but will become important as the story unfolds. Also not communicated to me was a subsequent conversation between my wife and Billy Bob revealing that he had three children from a previous marriage. As it turns out, neither the fact of his previous marriage nor the existence of his three other children was known to Melody either.

Bet you're not surprised. It's the nature of scorpions to

bite. So if you fool with scorpions, expect to be bitten.

But I'm getting ahead of myself. The conversation with Melody once I arrived went something like this:

MELODY: Billy Bob's in jail. I need you to get him out.

ME: He's in jail!!

MELODY: In Yenimsville (a three-hour drive from where we were sitting).

ME: I'm not a criminal attorney. I have no earthly idea how...

MELODY: He trusts you. You're his attorney! You have to do something.

ME: But...

MELODY: He's been there since...this is Wednesday...since last Thursday. Please, you have to get him out!

ME: What's he in there for? I mean, what happened?

MELODY: I don't know. He didn't say.

ME: But I'm not a...I know nothing about getting people out...I mean bail, going before a judge...nothing about...

MELODY: All I know is he trusts you. Here, I signed the retainer. That makes you his lawyer. Aren't you bound to help him?

Only Billy Bob's signature could have made me his attorney, and only in regard to his accident. But Melody wasn't leaving until I promised to do something.

ME: Okay. I'll see what I can do in the morning. It's too late to do anything tonight. (As I later realized, jails work $^{24}/_{7}$, so it's never too late.)

MELODY: Promise?

ME: I'll do what I can. I'll call you by noon.

New conversation. This time with a Deputy Sheriff of Yenim County, to whom I had been directed when I called the Yenimsville police department. I yet had no idea of what I needed to do, mainly because I didn't know why Billy Bob was in jail—or why he was being held so far from his home. This was a fact-gathering call.

DEPUTY: Can I help you?

ME: My name's David Tannenbaum. I'm an attorney.

DEPUTY: Never heard of you. What's your problem?

ME: I understand you are holding a client of mine.

DEPUTY: We're holding lots of lawyers' clients. What's the name?

ME: Billy Bob Johnson.

DEPUTY: What of it?

ME: What's he done? Why are you holding him?

DEPUTY: Sorry, counselor. I don't know who the hell you are. So until I do, you get nothing. You got my drift?

I vaguely recalled from law school—or some detective story—that the police cannot hold anyone beyond a certain period without a court order. At that point I didn't know the limit was twenty-four hours. But I just winged it.

ME: You've had him a week now. What judge ordered his retention? What's the bail?

DEPUTY (after a long pause): Give me your phone number and I'll let you know when he'll be arraigned.

ME (sensing a problem on their part): Did you just say you've held him a week without...

DEPUTY: I said I'll call you.

And the line went dead.

I ran to the library to look up arraignment times. That's when I found the twenty-four hour requirement for an arraignment before a judge. The statute used the word 'shall.'

Not good for the cops. Score one for the home team.

Back in my office, the phone rings. Deputy, who now knows my name, tells me to come get Billy Bob.

ME: What's the bail amount?

DEPUTY: Just pick him up. He's free to go.

And again the line goes dead.

I called Melody to tell her the news, but she informed me that Billy Bob had already been released.

ME: He's out already?

MELODY: He called me. They came and got him just after eight this morning. Told him to shave and get outside as fast as he could.

ME: That's...good. Go get him. How about having him come to my house tomorrow night so he can tell me what's going on.

MELODY: I can't thank you enough! You're the best! He'll be there.

Sure enough, Billy Bob showed up the next night.

BILLY BOB: You're the best lawyer ever! One call from you and they couldn't wait to get me out of that cell. What the hell did you say to them?

ME: They screwed up is all. What's this all about?

BB: You're my lawyer, right? I can talk in confidence?

ME (reluctantly): Yes.

BB: Before I started selling magazine subscriptions I managed a grocery store not far from here. Ordered the products, stocked the shelves, paid the bills, hired and fired, the whole nine yards. Owner was never around.

ME: Sounds like a good gig.

BB: I screwed up.

ME: Go on.

BB: Got in over my head in a card game. Owed a bunch of money I couldn't pay. The grocery store checkbook showed a large balance so I wrote out a few checks for phony made-up invoices. I think of it as I floated myself a loan.

ME: Translation: You voted yourself a bonus.

BB: Yeah. But the...the loan only lasted a few months before the bookkeeper caught me. They fired my ass and...

ME: ...filed criminal charges.

BB: Had me arrested for embezzlement.

ME: How much?

BB: Three grand.

ME: I don't get how you wound up in the Yenimsville jail. Should have been in this county. That's where you worked, right?

BB: I was arrested in this county on the check thing, but my prints came up on an old arrest in Yenim County.

ME: How old?

BB: When I was eighteen. In the service. Bunch of us on leave were out drinking. I was sleeping in the back seat. They went into a convenience store and stole a case of beer. Cops caught us two blocks away.

ME: That doesn't add...

BB: One of the guys had a gun. Might have taken some money as well.

ME: You convicted?

BB: Spent two nights in jail and never heard back from them.

ME: Service? Army?

BB: Yes.

ME: Honorable discharge?

BB: Yes.

ME: Any idea why you never heard from Yenimsville?

BB (looking at the carpet): Changed my name.

ME: I still don't get it. They would have found the old arrest warrant when you went to court for the name change.

BB: Had a spare birth certificate. I was adopted very young. Mother got unwantedly pregnant and left me at the firehouse as an infant. I took the name of the folks who raised me. After I got out of the service, I began using my birth name.

ME: Which is Billy Bob Johnson?

BB: Yes. It was Billy Bob Cormack before that.

ME: Anything before that?

BB: Other than Billy Bob Johnson, no.

ME: Embezzlement, robbery. I certainly am the wrong lawyer for you. I have no experience...

BB: You're the best, man. No one better. You sprung me with one phone call. Can't beat that! I don't want to hear you can't do it. You're doing it. Just keep doing it.

* * *

"And who are you?" the prosecutor asked when I walked into his cubicle-sized office two days later.

After I introduced myself as Billy Bob's lawyer the prosecutor dug through a pile of blue folders precariously piled on a chair beside his desk. He slipped one out, took a moment to scan several pages, dropped it on his desk, then looked up at me. "What the hell's a corporate type like you doing representing a crook like this??"

"It's a long story."

He reached for a pad of paper. "What's your office address? All I have in the file is your home address."

"As the file obviously shows, I'm a corporate lawyer, but I see clients at my home."

"You see criminal defendants in your home?"

"This one I do."

"Got a wife? Children?"

I confirmed that I did.

"Better watch them when he's around. No telling what felons are capable of. And while you're at it, better keep a close eye on the china and silverware."

"I'll keep that in mind. Let's talk about a plea deal. How about he pleads guilty, repays the money, and gets a suspended sentence." Isn't this how they do it on TV shows?

"You kidding me? Open and shut case. He signed the checks. Handwriting is a clear match. Have affidavits from several cashiers identifying Billy Bob as the man who cashed them. There are no extenuating circumstances. He's doing two to five."

"Cut me a break, will you? How about..."

"Only break you get is your choice of prison. Three to select from. And mind you, I can only make suggestions. Bureau of Prisons decides where to send prisoners."

"Not a good offer."

"You got no case. Plead and you pick the location, maybe. Go to trial and the wife will have to drive four hours to see him. No weekend visiting, so she'll have to take a day from work." When I didn't answer, the prosecutor said, "You have plenty of time to think about it. Trial won't be set for six months, maybe a year. Tell your client to enjoy his freedom—while he still has it."

A few months pass. I call Billy Bob perhaps ten times to schedule time to plan his defense. I am constantly put off with a statement extolling my prowess as a lawyer and his telling me that we have plenty of time. "Don't sweat the small stuff" seemed to be his life philosophy, combined with "you sprung me once, you'll do it again."

It was some four months after I first met Billy Bob that my phone rang. I was in the middle of a contract negotiation, and Billy Bob and his legal problems were as far from my mind as could be. In fact, when the prosecutor announced himself, I didn't recognize the name. "Be in my office in one hour," he instructed. "It's your lucky day. I'm prepared to take your offer."

"How about in the morning?" I countered. "Today's a busy day for me."

"One hour from now, sharp, counselor, or the deal's gone."

"Can't we do this on the phone?"

"In my office! At eleven. We're in court at one. Be certain your client is here by twelve-thirty."

As luck would have it, Billy Bob answered his home phone and promised to meet me at the courthouse at the appointed time. "Wear a jacket and tie," I advised. "And shave."

"Here's the drill," the prosecutor said when I entered his office. "In exchange for pleading guilty and making full restitution, your client gets a suspended one-year sentence. No probation.

Not believing what I was hearing, I made him repeat what he had just told me. Too good to be true is not what I ever expect, so I said, "How do I know that if Billy Bob pleads guilty the judge'll go along with what you just said? For all I know, he can throw the book at my client."

"That's a chance you just have to take."

"I have your word on this."

"For what it's worth, you do."

"Can he pay off the restitution over time?"

"No problem."

My first criminal case, a felony, begins in less than two hours. First things first. I call my wife to tell her.

She is sitting in the courtroom when Billy Bob and I walk in. That wasn't smart on my part. Sitting next to her is her sister.

When Billy Bob's case is called, the clerk asks my name. But the words that the clerk actually says are, "Appearance of counsel."

I was so preoccupied trying to figure out where Billy Bob and I were supposed to stand that I didn't realize what the clerk was asking. So I stood silent, causing the clerk to raise his voice to a level that carried to the back of the courthouse, "Please state your name for the record, counselor."

I heard this, but didn't realize until the prosecutor looked over at me, that the clerk had been addressing me. I stated my name.

"Speak up, counselor!" the judge barked. "The court reporter needs to hear. And please spell your last name."

Not off to a good start. Worse, my sister-in-law for years afterward would repeat and embellish that scene to the point where, in her tale of my first day in court, I sounded like an imbecile. In truth, however, that is precisely how I felt. Perry Mason I wasn't.

Formalities finally over, the judge looked at me, then at Billy Bob, then back to me. He seemed confused as to which of us was the lawyer and which the defendant. Not clearly making up his mind, he looked in our general direction, and said, "Billy Bob Johnson, you are charged with one count of embezzlement. If found guilty you could be subject to up to ten years in state prison. How do you plead?"

"The defendant pleads guilty," I mumbled, but in a voice loud enough to be heard. Then, remembering my John Sullivan years, I thought to add, "Your Honor." I felt good, because that's how they did it in the movies.

"I want the defendant to answer for himself," the judge admonished. "How do you plead, son?"

I leaned over and whispered, "Say guilty."

Billy Bob stood tall. "I did it. I'm guilty, judge."

He'll be lucky to get only ten years. I hope the bailiff figures out which one is the lawyer and which the defendant when it comes time to snap on the cuffs.

"Judge," the prosecutor said. "This is the matter we discussed yesterday. The gambling...situation."

"Oh, yes. I forgot there was one more. Okay." The judge consulted several sheets of paper before again looking in our general direction. "Since you have pled guilty in open court to one count of embezzlement, I hereby sentence you, Billy Bob Johnson, to one year imprisonment, the sentence suspended with no probation requirement."

The judge slammed his gavel and called for the next matter.

Billy Bob turned to me and asked, "How much do I have to pay a month for restitution?"

I started to ask the prosecutor, but luckily my brain engaged first. The judge hadn't mentioned restitution, so as it stood no restitution was required. Open my mouth and the judge could very well modify the order. "Let's get out of here," I said, grabbing Billy Bob's arm. "We can talk outside."

Billy Bob turned and followed me to the courtroom exit. With each step I expected the judge to wake up and call us back. But the heavy door closed behind us with nary a peep.

Once outside on the courthouse steps, Billy Bob threw his arms around me and thanked me, again proclaiming me the greatest lawyer who ever lived. "You're the best, man. The very best! No jail time, no probation, and I keep the money. Can't beat that."

For three days, even I believed I was a pretty good lawyer, if the measure of being a good lawyer is getting a guilty felon off with a suspended sentence and no court costs or restitution. In the criminal law field, I couldn't think of another criterion to measure by. So, okay, I was good.

But not that good!

Friday's newspaper headlines told the real tale. Only it still took me a day to understand what it all meant. The FBI had arrested twenty people on gambling, usury, and extortion charges, mostly stemming from rigged poker games. Seems as though crooked poker games were being used to hook "marks," and then money was loaned to the marks to repay the debt. Then to repay the loans, the marks ended up performing any one of a number of criminal activities, with Billy Bob's embezzlement being among the lowest level of the felonies. Buried in the article was the fact that several people, mostly marks like Billy Bob, had worn wires to gather evidence for the FBI in exchange for suspended sentences.

I had been clueless. Great lawyer indeed!

DIVORCE

(PhD Style)

An internal client in the company where I did my intellectual property work walked into my office and plopped into the only visitor's chair in my small room. His name was Jim.

"Nice carpet," he said. Not "Good morning, David," or "Do you have a moment?" or "How're you doin'?" Just "Nice carpet."

"Thanks, I guess," was all I could think to say.

Jim jumped right in.

"Listen, would you do a divorce for me?"

I had been to Jim's house for a party just the previous weekend. Everything seemed okay with the marriage. "For you and Jill?"

"Who else?"

"Seems a bit odd. I mean, the party and all."

"Our way of saying goodbye to everyone."

But they hadn't said any final goodbyes—or anything else to suggest that there was trouble in paradise.

"Really? I didn't hear anything about any divorce," I said. "And anyway, I don't know anything about divorce family law. You need a lawyer who specializes in divorces."

"They're too expensive."

"I'm not exactly cheap."

"There's no way you could charge as much as they do."

"Like I said, I'm not qualified for divorce."

"That's why you have to charge less. Besides, we have no kids. And Jill won't contest."

"And the grounds for this divorce are what?"

"Mental anguish."

"What?"

"As you may remember," Jim continued, "my degree is in psychology, and I know when people are playing mind games. She's degrading me."

"Okay," I said, already more than a little skeptical. "What's an example? I mean, an example of her degrading you?"

"Like driving. When I'm parking the car she's forever giving me instructions. 'Now cut the wheel left.' 'Go slower,' 'Speed up,' 'Watch that fender.' She makes me feel inadequate."

"Have you told her that?"

"No use. She won't stop."

"How about trying to talk it out?"

"Are you going to represent me or not?"

"I don't think you need a divorce lawyer. You need a..." I was going to say "psychologist" but realized the irony of that. "You need to talk with your wife," I offered. "Work it out."

"That's not an option." Jim stood as if to leave. But he didn't leave. "You going to do it or not?"

"You're sure you want a divorce?"

"Positive."

"You sure you want me?"

"A divorce is a divorce. As long as it's valid, that's all I care. Just don't screw it up. And I know that the price will be right. Right?"

"Well, let's see. How much are you thinking?"

"The guy on the corner charges six hundred. I thought two hundred would be fair."

Two hundred dollars was ridiculously low, of course, even back in the late 60s. But getting paid to learn new skills is never a bad deal, I told myself, but I countered on general principal. "Three hundred. Plus expenses."

"Deal."

This would be not only my first family law case, but my first civil case of any kind. I didn't even know where the domestic relations court was located, or anything about divorce law. The future portended lots of time in the law library.

Lucky me, or so I thought, the law in the state where Jim and I worked was going to change over in about six months to a "no fault" system. Under law still in effect, there were very few grounds for divorce, and mental cruelty was the only one that had even a remote chance of being applicable—and a big stretch at that. "From what little I know of the law," I told Jim, "Jill telling you how to park the car is not mental anguish. If it was, we'd all be eligible for divorce."

"To a psychologist it is! Put me on the stand and I'll set the judge straight."

Put him on the stand, I thought, and we'd both be doing thirty days in jail...for wasting the court's time.

"Let's just wait six months for the no-fault law to take effect."

"F--- that! Nope! Can't wait!"

Jim's violent response made me think that it might actually be mental anguish for Jim to stay married. But I didn't think the judge would see it that way.

Fast forward to one week before our appointed day in court. I drove the hour and half in rush hour traffic to be in the courtroom at eight forty-five so I could see how it all worked. The place was packed. At exactly nine, the bailiff pushed open the door, someone yelled, "All rise!" and everyone stood as a black robed, white-haired grandfather type entered through a side door and took his place behind a table on a raised podium.

He motioned us down and we all sat. So far, so good.

"What is that man doing in my courtroom?" the judge bellowed. "Get him out of here until he shows respect!"

The object of the judge's scorn was a hapless young man with hair hanging down over his shoulders in the back and a beard extending halfway down his chest in the front. From what I could determine, though, his "disrespect" stemmed from his being the only male in the room not wearing a jacket.

Note to self: Remind client to wear a suit.

The bearded man shuffled to the center aisle and then disappeared through the rear courtroom door.

The judge called the first matter. Jarndyce versus Jarndyce, or some such thing. After some preliminaries, the judge turns to the lawyer at plaintiff's table. "Call your witness."

"I call Mrs. Jarndyce."

Note to self: I can do this.

"No! No! No!" The judge shouts. His face red with rage. "That's even worse!"

We all turn to the back door, where the bearded young man has appeared in a leather jacket, complete with copper studs. The stunned man stammers, "That's all I have to wear!"

"You will not come into this courtroom in your biker get-up! Now get out until you dress properly!"

"But I need to testify...I..."

"One more word and you'll be in contempt, and in jail if you keep disrespecting this court!"

"But..."

"Bailiff!"

So much for Judge Grandfather.

A uniformed guard took the bearded man by the arm and shoved him into the hall.

Note to self: I don't want to be here. No way that giving parking instructions is going to constitute mental cruelty in this judge's mind. Better remember to bring my toothbrush.

Mrs. Jarndyce took the stand and the tales she told of her husband's physical abuse made me sick. Not only would I have granted a divorce, but if I had been the judge I would have locked up the assh---.

"Have you tried counseling?" the judge asked flatly, as if a wife-beating habit is something to be talked out of with a little chit-chat.

"Yes. But he continues to..."

"How long was the counseling?"

"I don't..."

"How many times did you see the counselor?"

"Once."

"Once is not enough. Try again. At least three sessions." The judge banged his gavel. "Next case!" he intoned.

"But he wouldn't go," the woman stammered.

"I said 'next case.' Counselor, control your client!"

Bailiff: "Matter number 0123679. Baker versus Baker. Child support, Your Honor."

A frightened woman who looked as though she hadn't eaten in a month came forward, accompanied by a bent-shouldered man, who I assumed was her lawyer. If anyone was to be thrown out of the courtroom for disrespect it should have been him. His suit was not only cheap and three sizes too large, but he appeared to have slept in it for weeks.

"Your Honor," the old guy wheezed, "we're here because Mr. Baker has refused to pay child support."

"Is Mr. Baker in court?"

"He was, Your Honor, until you threw...he was the man in the leather jacket."

"Well, whatever. Is he still around?"

"Here I am," a voice from the back announced. All eyes swung to the rear as the bearded man rose to his feet. He was now wearing a jacket that hung down to his mid-calves, with sleeves extending six inches beyond his fingers.

Snickers arose from the audience, only to be cut short by a sharp gavel bang. "Order in this court or I'll throw you all out!"

"What's your excuse for not paying child support?" the judge demanded, once Baker had been sworn in and seated in the witness chair.

"Lost my job. I tried to pay her what little I had but she refused. Now she wants more. I don't have no money."

"You have a bike to go with that leather jacket?"

"I do. Yes, sir."

"In the parking lot?"

"It is."

"Seize it, Bailiff! Go out there and lock that bike up. Mr. Baker, I will give you one week to pay what you owe or that bike will be sold. Understand me?"

"You can't take..."

"Yes I can. I just did. You want it back, pay up."

"I can't."

"Get a job! And next time you come to this court, dress properly. Now get out! Next case."

I had seen enough. I slid out of my seat and fell in beside the unkempt lawyer, both of us beating a hasty retreat from the insanity.

Grandfather indeed.

Three hours later, I had Jim in my office. "Trust me when I tell you the facts of your case will not support a divorce. My God, a man beating his wife was not enough!"

"I'll take my chances."

"If you insist. But this is a waste of money and time."

"I said go for it."

"Wear a suit and tie. And closed toe shoes. Those sandals won't cut it. Be there at 8:30."

To Jim's credit, he was on time and properly dressed. I think the shoes were new. At least he had listened. The roster of cases posted in the hall said that our case was second. Bearded Baker was on the list above us. I hadn't noticed if his bike was still locked down in the place I had seen it when I last left the courthouse.

"Baker versus Baker, matter number 0123679," the Bailiff announced, after the standing up/sitting down ritual was done with.

It was not quite the same Mr. Baker who appeared this time. The hair at the back of his head had been trimmed, the beard didn't seem as long, and he was now wearing a jacket that allowed his hands to show at the end of the sleeves.

The same slump-shouldered lawyer, this time without Mrs. Baker, but wearing the same suit, made his way to the table in front of the bench, holding a smudged envelope over his head. "Your Honor," he said, "I am pleased to report that just this morning Mr. Baker handed me this envelope containing all the money he owes plus enough for another month."

The judge sighed. "Very well. I suppose I'll have to unlock his bike, then. Too bad. The man needs to get a job and not ride around all day making a racket. So ordered."

"Rivers versus Rivers, matter number 0124387," the Bailiff called out.

Show time!

I dutifully marched to the front table, gave my name and address to the clerk and fell silent waiting for the boom to fall.

It didn't take long.

"Are you serious, counselor?" the judge scoffed. "Your client claims mental anguish because his wife helps him park the car?"

"I know it sounds far-fetched, Your Honor, but I actually am serious. I believe..."

"I don't care what you believe! Get your client sworn in."

I nodded to Jim to take the witness chair. Before he did, the Bailiff had him raise his right hand and, following the usual formula, asked him to swear to tell the truth "so help you God."

"Can we leave the God part out?" Jim asked.

"No!" the judge snapped. "Get on with it. Either say 'yes' or get out of here and stop wasting my time."

I had forgotten to tell Jim to pack a toothbrush. The jail bus was waiting for him and there was nothing I could do.

"Okay, then" Jim wisely conceded. "Yes."

"So, now. Let's get to it. You're telling the court that it's mental anguish for your wife to help you park the car?"

"Yes. I'm a Ph.D. in psychology, and her telling me things like that discredits my manhood and..."

"A Ph.D. huh? From where, if I may be so bold as to ask?"

"Harvard."

"They should rescind your degree. I never heard such crap in my life. It's what wives do, my young friend, and it goes with the territory. Didn't they teach you that at Harvard?"

"I know mental anguish when..."

"Enough! Get out of here! You can get your divorce when the law changes to no-fault, but not a day sooner. Not in my court. Next case."

I couldn't leave it at that. No, sir. After all, I was being paid to represent my client and I'd hardly said two words. "But, Your Honor, please listen to his argument. The man is the expert on mental anguish. If he says..."

"One more word from you, counselor, and you'll learn the hard way who the expert in this courtroom is. And I assure you it is not your client!"

To speak or not to speak? Actually, I saw the choice as being whether to spend the night in a jail cell or at home with my wife. I chose the latter and kept my mouth shut.

Eight months later Jim marched into my office waving his divorce decree, granted under the no-fault law.

"Did it myself. Piece of cake," he announced proudly, and before I could congratulate him, he added, "Saw the mess you made and figured I couldn't do any worse."

Jim resigned from the company shortly thereafter, and I never saw him again.

Mental anguish, huh? Most of the mental anguish in this case was my own. Not to mention that Jim never did pay my bill.

Mrs. Wiśniewski's Garage

(It's Not Our Policy)

"Mr T, is that you?"

"Yes. Who's calling please?"

"Mrs. Wiśniewski. Remember me?"

I did remember Mrs. W. Who wouldn't? She had been referred to me by a friend several years previously because her husband had been locked out of his job as a maintenance mechanic for a state-run project. He hadn't been able to punch in for four days, and on the fifth day he had been fired for unexcused absence. His union refused to help him because the guy who had locked him out was the union local representative and the husband had gotten tired of paying him off in order to work.

I advised Mrs. W to have her husband go to his boss and tell him his side of the story. The boss, as it turns out, had suspected that the shakedown scheme had been going on, but had no proof or corroboration until Mr. W came in, at which point, of course, he was given his job back.

First Mrs. W problem solved.

Second Mrs. W problem: Her detached garage had caught

fire and the insurance company refused to pay, claiming that the policy did not cover detached structures.

Mrs. W brought her copy of the policy to my home office, and it clearly showed the garage to be covered. A call from me to the insurance company produced a whole lot of coughing, sputtering, back-peddling, and frankly, outright lying, all ending with, "we'll look into it and get back to you."

Two weeks later, having not heard from the insurance company, I called again, asked to speak to the adjuster handling the case and, when he came on the line, I demanded that Mrs. W's claim be paid.

"That won't be happening," was the reply.

"Why not. The garage burned down?"

"They were using it for a bedroom."

That was a fact I hadn't known, but I pretended that I did. "So?" I said.

"So. The policy excludes garages used for sleeping quarters."

"Where's that in the policy?"

"Check it out, counselor. Article Three, Paragraph Four.

"I have the policy right in front of me," I said. "There is no Paragraph Four in Article Three."

"You have the wrong policy," came his reply.

"Really! Well the one I'm looking at is the one your company gave my clients when they signed up and the one they've been paying their premiums on for the past ten years. So now you're trying to pull a bait and switch, is that it? "

"Not at all."

"Well, does the policy cover the garage or not? The paper I have in front of me says it does."

"What are the numbers in the top right corner of the front page?"

"HO-3-2102

"You have the wrong policy."

"Really? How do you suppose that happened?"

"Whatever. It's the wrong one."

A sixth sense told me that there was more to the story than the adjuster was letting on and that this "wrong policy" claim was a subterfuge—indeed, a complete fabrication.

"There's something you're not telling me," I pressed. "Why don't you tell me what's really going on here?"

"Truth is," the adjuster said after a pause, "our investigators believe the fire was self-inflicted."

"Arson?"

"You can call it that."

"Have you notified the police?"

"No."

"I see. So here's what we're going to do. Listen carefully. You have twenty-four hours to file a formal complaint with the police or notify me that a check is in the mail in full payment of my client's claim. And here's the important part. If you do file a police report and there is no credible evidence of arson, my client will sue the insurance company for defamation as well as fraud. I am certain the insurance commissioner will be interested to hear what you have to say about not paying this claim. Bye now."

The check in the full amount arrived a week later.

Second Mrs. W matter solved.

"Of course I remember you, Mrs. W," I replied. "How's the patented wiper blade coming along?"

I was referring to the patent I had obtained for her. She had come up with the idea for her improved wiper blade when she had been driving on a toll road and it had begun to rain heavily as she was approaching a tollbooth. She turned on her wipers, only to find they had deteriorated to the point where they were useless. Because of the lack of visibility, she scraped her mirror on the toll bin. Her solution was to incorporate a device into the wiper blade that would sound a noise when the blade was no longer wide enough or flexible enough to do its job well. The driver would then know to replace the blade before it failed completely. "The way it is now," she had explained, "it fails when you need it most, when you first turn it on. With my invention, it tells you before it actually fails."

"I didn't call you about the patent. Not this time. I have a different problem."

"What can I help you with?"

"We're sitting around the kitchen table trying to figure out what to do and my husband says, 'Call that lawyer. He'll know.' So, can you help?"

"I'll try. What's up?"

"My father died."

"I'm so sorry to hear that. And...?"

"He was sitting here having a beer and he just fell over."

I still had no idea what the question was, but Mrs. W had fallen silent. I was gathering my thoughts, trying to get a sense of the timeline, and then asked if they had called an undertaker or the police.

"Oh! That's it! Thank you so much Mr. T. See? My husband was right to have me call you. I have to get off to call the undertaker."

The phone went dead.

David Harry Tannenbaum

Someone dies, and so you call the undertaker. If only all of life's problems were so easily solved.

THE JACKSONS

(Or Never Ask a Question You Don't Already Know the Answer to)

Attorneys in my state were assigned by the court system to handle minor criminal cases ("misdemeanors"), without compensation, when the accused person could not afford to hire a lawyer.

My corporate office was twenty miles from the courthouse, and my home was five miles in the other direction, so I had no convenient place to interview people I was assigned to represent. I had explained this to the judge as part of my petition to be excused from participating in pro bono work. "I'll tell you what, counselor," he had said, a twinkle in his eye. "You can use the clerk's office to meet with your assigned clients. I'll have the clerk vacate her office an hour before court so you can use it undisturbed. That sound fair to you?"

It sounded horrible to me. "Yes, Your Honor, I suppose that will work." And for the next six years it worked out well enough, but only if you regard an almost unblemished record of convictions (losses on my part) as working out well.

The Jackson case was one such "pro bono" matter, actually my first misdemeanor case, or something very close to it. It was a domestic disturbance incident, which cops hate. And for very good reason.

As told to me by Mrs. Jackson, her husband had arrived home about two in the morning with a load on or, as the British might say, Jackson toddled up the stairs in his cups. Gaining the landing, shoes in hand so as not to disturb the missus, he paused to allow his watery eyes to adjust to the dim light, only to discover that he's not alone. Mrs. Jackson was there to welcome him home—a frying pan at the ready. Apparently, the last time he came home in this condition, it had been he who had taken the frying pan to her.

Now the playing field had been leveled. Well, not exactly. Hubby weighed in at no more than 110 pounds dripping wet, while his bride tipped the scales at 200 or so and was a foot taller.

The fight began immediately. Who started the verbal barrage we'll never know. Who it was that landed the first blow is likewise lost to history. At some point, a neighbor rang up the police—no doubt using speed dial because of the numerous previous incidents. A lone officer arrived four minutes later.

The officer made his way up the stairs, and when he arrived near the top—according to the wife's version of the story—her husband, reeling from a well-placed blow of the frying pan, staggered backward out of the door and stumbled down the top step. Instinctively, the officer reached out to prevent Jackson from falling all the way down the flight of stairs. Unfortunately, a knife the husband had been clutching in his fist cut the officer's forearm. Hence the arrest of Mr. Jackson for assault of a police officer in the line of duty.

The offense was charged as a misdemeanor (a crime carrying a maximum penalty of less than a year in jail), qualifying it to be handled by an assigned pro bono attorney, which turned out to be me, my name having reached the top of the list once again. Assaulting a police officer actually ought to have been charged as a felony (more than a year in jail), and I never understood how it came to be charged instead as a misdemeanor. If it had been charged as a felony, the case would have been handled by the full-time public defender instead of by assigned counsel like me. But while I might have wished for the assault to be upgraded to felony status, procedurally (not to mention ethically) that would not have been possible.

My interview with Mrs. Jackson further revealed that she was tired of being pushed around by her husband and tired of his drinking, so she had started this fight by hitting him a few times, "somewhere up around his stupid thick head. I wanted to teach him a lesson. Fool grabbed a knife from the table, but he was too far gone to use it. I hit him again and that's when he ran out of the kitchen. Cop was there and got cut. The stupid jerk was in no condition to even know what he was doin'."

Here was the problem: If the husband went to jail, he would lose his job. The wife earned very little from her job. Then they wouldn't be able to make the rent and would have to move. So, the wife had every reason to play up the incident as an accident, rather than as a willful attack on an officer. And while I therefore had good reason to disbelieve her version of the events, the real question was how I was going to convince the judge that it happened the way she said.

I had no answer.

Once we were in court, the cop took the stand. He testified that he was on his way up the steps. Heard shouting and banging. The defendant came flying out of his door and ran down the steps. The officer told him to put his hands up, whereupon defendant pulled a knife and slashed the officer's arm.

The officer then paused in his testimony, reaching into a shopping bag to produce a blue shirt with two neat cuts across the right sleeve. He pointed to a dark area on the sleeve.

"That's my blood, right there," he announced. "Took four stiches to close it up."

The judge turned to me. "Any questions for the officer, Mr. Tannenbaum?"

I stood, recalling what the wife had told me. "Officer," I begin, "was the defendant running down the steps, or was he falling?"

"Running."

"Could he have tripped?"

"He could have, but he didn't. He was running."

"Was he facing toward you, or was his back to you?"

"He was coming down the steps."

"No further questions, Your Honor," I announced, unable to think of anything further to ask. The hole was already deep enough. Time to stop digging.

"Okay, counselor, the officer is excused. You may call a witness if you wish."

This was not going to end well. There was no question the officer had been cut. There was also no question my client did the cutting. The only question was the husband's intent. And only one or the other of the Jacksons could provide any clue as to that.

"I call Mrs. Jackson."

While the wife was making her way to the stand I studied the long list of questions I had written on my yellow pad. I continued reading the questions even while Mrs. Jackson was being sworn in.

My eyes remained on my pad as I heard her say, "I do," followed by the rustle of Mrs. Jackson taking her seat in the witness box.

"Mrs. Jackson," I asked, my head still down so as not to lose my place on the all-important pad, "are you married to the defendant, Wilbur Jackson?"

In my mind, I heard Mrs. Jackson answer in the affirmative. My head was still down while my finger moved to question number two. My mouth started to move, but it froze before a sound escaped.

Mrs. Jackson hadn't actually said yes. In fact, she hadn't said anything. Slowly I looked up at her.

"I...I...Oh, I am so...so embarrassed," she said, her head down.

How I had managed to embarrass my own client I had no idea. But she was clearly uncomfortable, to say the least. Sweat beaded on her broad forehead, and she appeared to be about to pass out.

"What is it, Mrs. Jackson?"

"Do I have to answer? I mean here in public with all these people? This is so bad, I...I mean, confessing my sins here... here in public."

"Answer the question, please," the judge said, leaning toward the witness.

"Oh, you see, we never did...me...and Wilbur we just...run off. Told everyone we was married. But we had no money... we just...lived together in sin. I always planned on making it legal but...but never got 'round to it." She looked up at the judge. "Will I...am I in trouble for saying that here in this court room, here with all these people. Did I do wrong?"

"No," I said to Mrs. Jackson. "It's okay to say that. You are okay. You are just telling the truth."

"Thank you. I promise we will be married as soon as... as we can."

"Now, Mrs. Jackson, I..."

"Freeman. I've been called Mrs. Jackson so long now I forgot. My real name is..."

"Jackson," the judge said. "We'll continue to call you Mrs. Jackson. You may tell your story."

"Mrs. Jackson," I began again, "tell the judge what happened that night. Tell him what you told me."

Mrs. Jackson then proceeded to relate the same story she had told me, including the part where Wilbur, reeling from a blow from the frying pan, fell down the steps, the knife cutting the arm of the officer in the process.

When she was finished, I said, "That's all I have, Your Honor. I believe Mrs. Jackson is telling the truth, and I believe Officer Henderson just didn't realize the defendant had tripped."

"You know, counselor, I must say I believe Mrs. Jackson. For her to confess she hadn't managed a marriage license apparently took a lot of courage. She didn't have to tell us that, but clearly she was incapable of lying. I find her to be a truthful woman, and I believe her account. I think Officer Henderson just didn't see the defendant trip, and the officer getting cut was an unfortunate accident. I find the defendant, Wilbur Jackson, not guilty."

The case proved to be one of my very few pro bono wins, thanks to Mrs. Jackson. And to think that I never got beyond question one on my pad.

BILLY BOB

(Part Two)

"Is this Lawyer Tannenbaum?" asked the raspy female voice on the other end of the line. I had just arrived at my office and hadn't even unlocked my desk. I acknowledged it was I, but before I could ask who was calling, the voice instructed me to "please hold for the district attorney."

Silence followed. Long enough of a silence for my mind to switch into high gear. District attorney? Which one? Why? I didn't have any criminal matter pending. In fact, no cases pending in any court anywhere. District Attorney? Grand jury jumped to mind. No one ever wants to field a call from the district attorney. It's never good news. Then the word indictment suggested itself. I live a boring life, so unless walking into a building through an EXIT door is a criminal offense, I can't imagine what a district attorney would want with me. So, then, what did I do wrong to attract the attention of some district attorney?

Enough time elapsed before the DA himself came on the line for me to have indicted myself, been tried, convicted, and sentenced to hard labor.

It was a deep male voice. "Is this Mr. Tannenbaum?"

My impulse was to respond "not guilty!" but thankfully I answered more rationally. "Yes. What's this about?"

"This is Robert Williams, district attorney of Blankenship County."

Anything you say can and will be used against you in a court of law, I told myself. "Can't say as I've ever even been in your county," I responded, congratulating myself on being totally non-committal. Deny everything.

"This is a courtesy call. Do you represent a man by the name of Billy Bob Johnson?"

Deny everything! Wait! Did he just say Billy Bob? Of course he had said Billy Bob. But I needed time to shift gears. Focus!

"Did you hear me? Is Mr. Johnson a client of yours?"

"He was," I replied. "I guess he still is. What did he..."

"I'm sorry to have to tell you that Mr. Johnson was found dead early this morning. Preliminary report indicates he took his own life."

"Oh, my!" The questions flooded in. "Where? How?"

"Police officer found his car parked off the side of the road. In a field, actually. A plastic tube ran from the exhaust pipe into the car. Windows rolled up. No evidence of foul play. Your name was written on a piece of paper in the passenger seat. No other identification."

"How do you know it was him, then?"

"Car registration in the name of his wife. She lives a good fifty miles from here. Officer from her city is with her now."

"Thank you for calling me," I said, not knowing what else to say.

"Not a hundred percent altruistic on my part, actually. It would be a big help if you could instruct Mrs. Johnson to cooperate and answer questions so I can get this case closed out and off my desk. I could then see to it that the body is released by the end of the day, no later than noon tomorrow."

"And if she doesn't want to answer questions?"

"Your Mr. Johnson might not get into the ground for a month or two. Who knows?"

I wanted to say more, but my other line was flashing. "I'll see what I can do."

"Mr. T?" It was the crying voice of Melody. "Billy's gone!"

"I'm so sorry. What..."

"We can talk privately later. Cops are here and they have questions for me. Should I answer them?"

How would I know? "Can they hear you right now?"

"I told them I was calling my lawyer so they're outside."

"What do you know about..."

"He killed himself!"

"How...?"

"He's been gambling again. Really heavy. He owes over ten thousand dollars. I just had a baby. Three weeks old yesterday. I found a note in his drawer that said..." She blew her nose several times. "...that said that unless he paid in full, the baby..." Sniffling, followed by heavy crying.

I waited. There was nothing I could say. It sickened me to anticipate what I thought I would hear next.

More sniffling, then, "Oh, my God...my God, the note said the baby wouldn't live another week! Oh, my God, Billy Bob killed himself to save the baby!"

When her crying stopped I told her what the DA had told me about cooperating.

"I can't bear not to bury him. Thinking of him in an ice locker somewhere..." Sobs, nose blowing, more sobs. "I have nothing to hide."

"Okay, then, tell them what you know. I'll work on getting him released, hopefully later today. You'll need a funeral home. So pick one and let the DA's office know who will be picking up the body."

"Oh, and the car as well," she said. "I can't afford to rent one and I'm told they plan to keep mine for weeks. I don't know how I'll get around."

Getting the body released proved easy. The DA had been bluffing. By the time I called him back arrangements had already been made with the funeral home. "Coroner's work was finished," is what I was told. "The DA sees no reason to inconvenience the family any further. No need to make this a bigger tragedy than what it already is."

But the car proved more difficult. The DA insisted that the car remain in evidence pending a hearing yet to be scheduled. In the end, they agreed to deliver the car to the wife by noon the next day. That was the best I could do. I told myself that at least dealing with the DA's office was now (hopefully) behind us.

The logistics of the following are a bit baffling, but they are what they are. Around eight p.m. the next night I received a frantic call from Melody. She was calling from a gas station pay phone. "Police!" the borderline hysterical voice sobbed. "Police made us leave!"

It took a few minutes before I learned that another woman, Janet, had shown up at the funeral home, looked in the open casket and screamed, "Hank!" The woman insisted that the man in the casket was her first husband, Hank Cormack. She had never heard the name Billy Bob but insisted that it was Hank Cormack who was about to be buried. How she knew he had died, I never did figure out.

"The funeral director called the police and when they showed up they emptied the funeral home and told me the funeral tomorrow was off until they got to the bottom of this.

They don't know how long it will take. I can't just leave my husband there, he needs to be buried tomorrow. My mother is on a bus on her way here and she has to go right back after the funeral. She can't afford to be missing work!"

"What do you know about this Hank Cormack?" I asked, remembering something about the name Cormack.

"Nothing. Nothing at all."

"Who is the woman who..."

"Never heard of her before. She says she was married to Billy...Hank...before me. I don't know what she's talking about!"

"Go on home. You have a ride? I'll call the police and see what I can find out."

"He has to be buried tomorrow. Oh, God, what a mess."

After confirming which town the funeral home was in I hung up. Melody was right. This was a mess. A gigantic mess by anyone's standards.

The first thing the police chief said when he came on the line was, "Thank God you called! That Billy Bob Johnson... Hank Cormack...situation is a mess. I understand you represent Billy Bob's, or whatever's his name, wife. That right?"

"Best as I can tell. What do you know about the other woman?"

"You mean, Janet Cormack?"

"I don't know who I mean. The woman who claims the dead guy's her former husband."

"Name's Janet Cormack and far as we can tell, she checks out. Lives a ways from here, but she's who she claims she is."

"Mrs. Johnson says you put a hold on the funeral."

"Nothing else I could do. Can't allow the wrong body to be buried. What a scene that was. Thought those two women would kill each other. It's a public safety issue now."

"I'm thinking that your real concern is knowing who is buried in that grave."

"You got that right. Digging up dead bodies is not my thing. He ain't going in the ground until I know positive who's down there. I don't want no fights either, you get my meaning?"

I got his meaning all right. But I also didn't think he had the right to stop a funeral. But who was I to debate the law with the man whose job it was to uphold the law. "How about this? Go over tonight, or early in the morning, and take a good set of prints. Match the prints and then we'll know."

"You know, that ain't a half bad idea. Melody Johnson wants him buried tomorrow and Janet Cormack doesn't at all care, except she wants to know for certain that the guy we bury is her former husband. A good set of prints will settle that matter once and for all. Tell your client the funeral can proceed as planned."

"Thank you, chief. Oh, and will you tell Mrs. Cormack not to show up at the funeral?"

"Trust me, she won't be there. I'll have officers stationed to keep the peace in case she does. Good idea, the prints. We'll let you lawyers—or the courts—sort it out later. Least we'll know who in the Sam Hill's been buried where."

What the chief didn't say, thank goodness, was that his plan for taking prints was to take the fingers themselves. He clearly did not have authority to mutilate a corpse, regardless of the reason. But try telling that to a police chief in the sixties.

Billy Bob, as I later learned, minus his fingers, was laid to rest the next day in what Melody told me afterward was a nice quiet dignified ceremony. Pastor and all.

Okay, so was it Billy Bob Johnson or Hank Cormack who Melody and her mother lowered into the ground? Well, if your money's on Billy Bob, you win. But if your money had been on Hank then you would have also won.

"How can that possibly be?" Melody asked when I informed her of the fingerprint results a few days later." I buried Billy Bob!"

Well, it seems some lives just aren't linear. Billy Bob Johnson is the name our hero was born with. But it seems he was left in a firehouse when he was a month or so old. A family by the name of Cormack adopted him and from that time until the name Cormack grew too hot to handle, he was known as Hank Cormack.

He went into the service as Hank Cormack. He was discharged and married as Hank Cormack. He disappeared from his wife and three children as Hank Cormack. He even robbed a liquor store as Hank Cormack. I didn't mention that he had told me a slightly different story leaving out the 'Hank' part. As the old adage has it, scorpions will be scorpions.

Time for a new life. He simply called the State Bureau of Vital Statistics, gave them his real birth information and lo and behold a shiny birth certificate in the name of Billy Bob Johnson arrived at his hideout flat. And off he went. Soon thereafter he wooed a young woman by the name of Melody.

"So let's go over the timeline again," I said to Melody while trying to get my head around the name changes of her deceased husband. "You say you and Billy Bob moved to Pennsylvania. When was that?"

"June 3rd of 1960."

"You were married when?"

"May 15th. Here in New Jersey. Church wedding, the whole nine yards."

"Same year?" I asked, shuffling the papers I had received from the state showing Hank Cormack's marriage and subsequent divorce from Janet.

"Yes, same year. 1960. Just before we moved. Here," she

said, handing me her marriage license duly issued by the State of New Jersey.

"That presents a bit of a problem, Melody," I said trying, but failing miserably, to break the news gently. "From the records I have here it appears your husband's divorce from Janet wasn't final until January 1961. That's after you married Billy Bob."

"Was I married at all?"

"I'm afraid not," I replied. "A marriage isn't valid if one of the partners is married to someone else at the time. So despite the marriage license and the nice words the minister spoke, despite exchanging rings and the 'I now pronounce you husband and wife,' despite the beautiful wedding gown and the tux Billy Bob rented, despite the champagne, the toasts and the great food, despite the dance band and the promises to cherish and obey, and even despite cutting and eating the wedding cake, the fact is, Melody, that at the end of the day you remained single while Billy Bob remained married to wife number one."

"If we weren't married, is he the father of my two children?"

"Yes, he's the father" I answered, it not being my place to say to Melody that only she would know who the father was. "But the honest answer to your marital question is that I'm not one hundred percent sure what your marital status was on the day he died. All we know for certain right now is that on the day after your marriage ceremony the two of you were not married—at least not to each other."

"That can't be! If we weren't married I won't get Social Security and I have two babies to raise! What will I do? I have no money. And all our credit cards are maxed out!"

"Let me work on it and see what I can find out." What I didn't say—because I was unsure of the exact wording of the law — was that unless I missed my guess, Social Security would be making payments to his first three children. Why else would Janet have shown up at the funeral home other than to protect that income stream? "You say your credit cards are maxed out. Send me the bills as they come in and I'll see what I can do."

"The store bills as well. We owe for everything."

"The store bills as well," I replied. In for a dime, in for a dollar.

To say that Melody left my home in a state of despair and confusion is to state the obvious. Not that I was much less confused than she. The facts as I knew them kept playing in my mind, starting with the fact that Billy Bob was married to Janet at the time of his marriage to Melody. And to compound the problem, he had three children by the previous wife. To further compound the problem, his divorce from the previous wife had occurred after his sham marriage to Melody. When Billy Bob departed this world he left behind Melody, as well as five children, one barely a month old, and a pile of debt. And an ex-wife claiming that her three children were entitled to share in the Social Security survivor benefits.

The debts, as it turns out, were the easy part of the situation, and actually proved to be a minor blessing. I had returned each bill in its payment envelope along with a copy of Billy Bob's death certificate. My hope was that the credit holders would just go away. But it was better than that. Almost every creditor (and I don't believe this is legal anymore for good reasons) as part of the fees they charged each month, had added in life insurance. Some policies paid off exactly what was owed. Some (with higher monthly fees) paid the highest balance over a six-month period. Some (with even higher monthly fees) paid the full credit amount even though that amount had not been charged. And some (by really gouging the borrower) charged for enough life insurance to cover twice the credit limit. In this situation, Melody received a windfall—close to five thousand dollars over and above what was actually owed. So three cheers for the questionable trade practice of charging credit borrowers for life insurance.

I turned my attention to the marriage question. As it turns out, Pennsylvania was one of only sixteen states that recognized common law marriages at that time. The rules to establish the existence of a common law marriage are (or were during the time Billy Bob and Melody lived there) that 1) a male and female couple, 2) neither with an impediment (such as being married to someone else), 3) intend to be presently married, 4) consummate the marriage, 5) hold themselves out as husband and wife, and 6) produce a witness who can attest to requirements 3, 4 and 5.

Requirements 1, 2 and 3 were a "go" for Melody. And I had to assume that having two children proves requirement 4—consummation. I had no idea what requirement 5 meant and I hoped number 6 would prove doable, assuming we could meet requirements 4 and 5. After extensive library time, and a dozen phone calls to various lawyers, I was ready to probe Melody for the facts.

ME: After Billy Bob's divorce, whose name was on the mailbox?

MELODY: We were married, or so I thought. So all our mail came addressed to Mr. and Mrs. Johnson, or to Mr. Billy Bob Johnson, or to Mrs. Melody Johnson.

ME: After Billy Bob's divorce—that is, after January 1961— did you introduce yourselves as being husband and wife?

MELODY: Of course. All the time.

ME: Can you come up with someone who saw you living together in your home as husband and wife? Someone who saw mail delivered with your married name? Someone who saw Billy Bob's clothes in the house, that kind of thing?"

MELODY: Would the minister do? He was in our home twice. Once after our first child was born and the second...

ME: When was your first child born?

MELODY: Strange question. Christmas. December 25th, 1961. Why?

ME: It means that the baby was conceived after Billy Bob became free to legally remarry. The minister is perfect. Did he sign a baptism certificate or something like that?

MELODY: Of course. I have it filed away. One of the few things, other than my first born, I have from that period of my life in fact.

ME: Congratulations! I don't think it's appropriate to offer a toast, but I hereby declare you and Billy Bob married under the common law of the Commonwealth of Pennsylvania.

Wonder of wonders, it only took the Social Security lawyers three weeks after receiving my memorandum and affidavits to declare Melody to have been married under the common law of Pennsylvania and therefore now a proper widow of Billy Bob and entitled to surviving spouse benefits. Melody's two children, however, had to share their surviving child benefits with Janet's three.

Not a bad outcome, though, considering the circumstances.

RAYMOND SMITH

(His Day In Court)

The story of Raymond Smith is the story of countless millions down on their luck (or more accurately, totally luckless) who spend their entire lives in and out of the justice system. They bounce from one caper to another in an endless march through lives that hold little promise of anything better.

Raymond Smith was still sitting in a jail cell a week after he backed a car over a police officer as he was leaving a shopping center parking lot. "It was an accident," Smith exclaimed as I sat down across from him. "Didn't see the jerk standing behind me. Should have gotten outta the way!"

"When you hit him what did you do?"

"Stopped! What the hell should I have done?"

"Okay. How did you know to stop? Did he yell? You feel something? Hear something?"

"All of that, man. Of course he yelled. Yelled pretty good."

"Says here, you left the scene. What's that about?"

"Guy's yelling and stuff. I got outta there."

"The officer's notes say they brought you to the station."

"Jerk must have called it in. Cops grabbed me a block away."

"So what else do I need to know?"

"Nothin' much."

"I'm going to read from the officer's notes. Stop me when I read something that's not true. You okay with that?"

"Go, man. I'm listenin'."

"You backed a car out of a parking spot in a lot. Cop was in uniform. You backed into him. Knocked him down. Your left back tire stopped on his ankle. You ran away leaving the car on his ankle. Two uniformed officers caught up with you at Hudson and Main. You had no driver's license. You had no insurance. You did..."

"Why the hell would I have insurance? I don't own a car."

"The car you were driving was..."

"Not mine."

"Whose then?"

"How the hell should I know?"

"Not a friend's?"

"Got no friends."

"I'll continue reading the notes. As I said, stop me when I say something that's not true."

"You didn't own the car. You didn't have permission to drive the car. The cop's ankle was broken and required being set."

"Serves the pig right!"

"I'm hard put to think of a defense for you. Any witnesses?"

"You think I'm stupid enough to, um, borrow a car with people lookin'?"

"How about pleading guilty and asking for time served?"

"I ain't pleadin' to nothing, man! I'm entitled to my day in court, and that's what I want! Nothin' less!"

"You got any idea what defense I can use?"

"Man, you the lawyer here. Ain't a good one either, from what I'm seein'."

"What about bail?"

"Got no money."

"Anyone to vouch for you?"

"Got no one. I told ya that already!"

"Okay. See you in court."

Raymond Smith got his day in court. The prosecutor put three police officers on the stand, one of whom was wearing a cast on his right ankle. Their sworn stories matched their written reports perfectly.

No cross-examination from me.

Putting Raymond on the stand was useless, but he wanted to tell his story. It couldn't help, and it could hurt. But he insisted that I let him have his day in court.

No surprise that he was found guilty as charged.

"Thanks, man," Raymond said to me as the bailiff escorted him back to his jail cell. "You did what you could. File an appeal. I'm entitled to an appeal."

The guy knew the system better than I did. He was right, and the fact that he had no money meant the state would foot the cost for appeal.

The only good thing as far as I was concerned was that I wouldn't have to handle the appeal which, in these circumstances, would be essentially a new trial in the county court. I simply had to file the notice of appeal and allow the machinery of state to take over from there.

That's the way it works—on paper at least. But not always in real life, as I discovered to my chagrin.

Flash forward three months. I'm sitting at my corporate office desk. It's ten-fifteen and the phone rings.

ME: Hello, David here.

VOICE: This is Judge Laurence Hildebrand. Tell me why I shouldn't hold you in contempt for not appearing in my courtroom this morning at nine o'clock?

ME (thinking it was a colleague pranking me, since the only court work I ever did was pro bono and I had nothing pending at the moment): Aren't you supposed to tell me to pack my toothbrush and kiss my wife goodbye? What kind of judge are you anyway?"

VOICE: Counselor! Just who do you think you are speaking to?

ME (as a sickening feeling worked its way from the bottom up): Who did you say you were?

VOICE: Judge Laurence Hildebrand. And you are David Harry Tannenbaum. Is that not correct, counselor?

I don't know if he convinced me with the "counselor" part. But certainly when I heard my middle name I was all ears—and stammers.

ME: Your Honor, I didn't know I was supposed to be in your court...

JUDGE HILDEBRAND: Son, you want to stay in practice you better get yourself a better docketing system. You were scheduled for nine this morning. It's now almost ten thirty. You better get trucking!

ME: I have no idea what...why...I have nothing...

JUDGE HILDEBRAND: The Smith matter. State versus Raymond Smith. Appeal from Municipal Court.

ME: I don't have a...Raymond Smith! That's the guy who ran over a cop! Your Honor, that's an appeal from...

JUDGE HILDEBRAND: That's what I just said! Appeal from...

ME: But, sir...Your Honor...I handled the original case pro bono. The state handles the appeal, right?

JUDGE HILDEBRAND: You're not the state-appointed lawyer on the appeal?

ME (seeing light at the end of this, but still thinking of my toothbrush): No, Your Honor. If I had been appointed, I would surely have been in court this morning.

JUDGE HILDEBRAND: Hold on a moment, counselor.

I'm holding on while listening for laughter at my door, still not a hundred percent convinced my fellow lawyers weren't setting me up. After all, it wasn't that long ago that I played one myself. The lawyer in the next office, Brian, had been assigned to a pro bono matter in which the defendant had become a bit rowdy in a motel room and smashed the furniture before the police arrived to escort him to jail. My prank was simple. I called Brian pretending to be security from the front lobby of our building. I informed Brian that a man who identified himself as a client of his was in the lobby. I instructed Brian to hurry because the fellow was busting up the lobby furniture. Brian was halfway to the lobby before it dawned on him that he had heard laughter in the hallway when he had come racing out of his office. I had been expecting retaliation ever since.

Five minutes went by, then eight. With every minute I became more convinced a prank was being played. But the stakes were too high to take any chances.

JUDGE HILDEBRAND: Sorry to take so long. I do owe you an apology. It appears the state forgot to assign this case out, and no one was notified of the hearing date. Now I have a problem, and perhaps I can ask a favor of you.

ME: Certainly, Your Honor. What is...

JUDGE HILDEBRAND: I have the defendant Smith in a holding cell downstairs and three police officers wasting their precious time. I want this case heard today. Would you consent to represent him?

ME: Today?

JUDGE HILDEBRAND: Yes, today.

ME: I am not prepared, Your Honor.

JUDGE HILDEBRAND: You are just as much prepared today as you were three months ago. Just present the facts as they are.

ME (feeling the noose tighten and helplessly scrambling for a way out): My office is over an hour away from the courthouse. I don't...

JUDGE HILDEBRAND: It's close to eleven now. Hour drive makes it twelve. I'll set it for one o'clock.

ME: But...

JUDGE HILDEBRAND: See you at one, counselor. Got a full afternoon. Don't be late.

The judge had spoken. I went out into the hall for one last sweep to be certain this was for real. All was in order. Prank or not, I was heading for my car. It was easier to live down a good prank than it was fighting to remain a member in good standing of the state bar. Not to mention spending time in jail on a contempt charge. While I was waiting for Hildebrand to come back on the line I had looked him up in the state bar directory. Just my luck. He was not just any judge. He was the county's chief judge. And had been for over twenty years. Not a man to fool with.

The hour drive went by all too fast. Said another way, I wasn't any closer to figuring out a defense for Raymond Smith at the end of the drive than I had been at the beginning. For that matter, I wasn't any closer than I had been three months earlier when the municipal court judge had found his sorry butt guilty as charged.

"You made it on time, counselor, thank you," Judge Hildebrand said when I tentatively poked my head into his chambers shortly before the appointed hour. "Judge McDonald is going to hear the case. His courtroom is on the fifth floor. Better hurry; he plans to start promptly at one."

I glanced at my watch. I had less than five minutes. "I haven't really had time to prepare. Can't this be adjourned, even a day?"

"Son, I'm familiar with the transcript. The man's guilty. Last time you put him on the stand. This time don't put him on the stand. Either way, the outcome'll be the same. Guilty is guilty. You'll get the same result tomorrow or the next day — or a year from now. Smith stole the car, ran over the cop, and left the scene. Nothing is in dispute. Now get up there and get this over with."

"Yes, sir...Your Honor."

"Oh, and when you're finished come back here. You and I have some unfinished business. Now get going."

Unfinished business. Like contempt of court for not showing up at 9:00? Do I at least get to make one phone call? My mind should have been on Smith's defense as I took the steps two at a time in a rush to be on time to McDonald's courtroom two flights up. Instead, I was working on my own defense. Keeping my license to practice was foremost on my mind.

"All rise!" the bailiff shouted as I pushed open the massive door to McDonald's court. "State versus Raymond Smith," McDonald, a slip of a man, announced in a voice surprisingly deep enough to shake the pews. "Is the state ready?"

"State's ready," came a faint female voice from the front of the courtroom.

"Is defense counsel ready? I understand there was a...a misunderstanding earlier with defense counsel. Has that been cleared up?"

"Defense counsel's here, Your Honor," I called as loud as I could muster as I quickly scurried down the aisle to the front.

"Speak up! Is counsel ready?"

"Ready," I replied, pushing my way through the swinging gate separating the counsel tables from the spectators—the few that there were. Or as ready as I ever will be for this matter. The names of several attorneys come to mind for my first telephone call after Judge Hildebrand locked me up.

"Proceed then. File your appearances."

I didn't do anything wrong, so how do I..."Nancy Somename for the state. Ready to proceed." ...get out of...

"And for the defendant?" The judge's booming voice cut through my thoughts.

"David Tannenbaum, Your Honor, for Mr., um, the defendant." His name had escaped me.

"Proceed."

At least the State goes first. Pay attention, David. Having one judge on your case is enough. Don't add a second one.

Attorney Somename called the same three police officers who had testified at the original trial. Their testimony was exactly as I had recalled it, with the only difference being the first cop walked to the stand without a cast, but this time with a pronounced limp.

I leaned over to Raymond Smith, who didn't appear any different than he had the last few times I had seen him. "How about this time not taking the stand? Didn't go well for you last time."

"I got an alibi this time."

"An alibi?" Now I have a mess. I am unprepared to put on alibi evidence. This is disbarment for certain. "What's the alibi?"

"I stole the wrong car. I should have stolen a smaller car. I couldn't see outta that hunk of junk."

"That's not an alibi. You'll be better off if you say nothing."

"I want to tell the judge my alibi."

"I don't advise it!"

"I want a new lawyer!"

"You got me."

"I don't want you. You a loser. Get me someone who'll let me tell my side of it!"

"Okay. Have it your way," I said, recalling Judge Hildebrand's lecture about him being found guilty no matter what I did. "Defense calls the defendant, Mr. Raymond Smith." I used his name so the record would show I at least knew who my client was.

"You should have done what?" the judge bellowed when Smith offered his alibi. "You were originally sentenced to eleven months. I should add a year to that sentence on general principal. Lucky for you the law doesn't allow that. I find you guilty as charged. Sentence remains the same. Clerk, see to it that the defendant is given credit for time served so far, including back to the day of his arrest, and remand him to the county jail to serve the remainder of his sentence. Next case."

Thankful that the case the bailiff called next was not State versus Tannenbaum, I left the courtroom to keep my date with destiny—in the form of Chief Judge Laurence Hildebrand.

"I'm told Smith was convicted," the judge said to me when I arrived. "He's well known in the system, you know. Been in and out, mostly in, since he was fourteen. The first time I had the pleasure of sentencing him it was for purse-snatching on his seventeenth birthday."

"How'd you remember him? With all the cases you've heard, they must..."

"His alibi. He claimed it was his mother's purse. He was just trying to get it back for her."

"Nothing's changed, I'm afraid. Criminal justice system has failed him," I replied, wishing I were anywhere other than in Hildebrand's chambers, and fearful that at any moment the bailiff was going to appear and lead me away. And me without my toothbrush. Root canal without painkiller was looking mighty good as an alternative.

"Actually it's life that has failed him. We do our best to protect society, but sometimes even our best isn't good enough." Judge Hildebrand sat back, looked over his desk at me, then said, "But I know you're wondering why you're here. It's only that I owe you an apology for speaking to you as I did earlier in the day when I called. You were right in thinking I was playing a prank, or whatever you thought. I want to make it up to you. Is there any favor I can do for you?"

I had no cases pending in county court, nor was I likely to have any. "No, Your Honor, there isn't."

"If you think of anything, I owe you one."

"Thank you." Better get out of Dodge while the gettin' is good. I got up to leave. Then I had a brain storm. "Oh, I just thought of something. Would it be too much to ask if my pro bono assignments are generated from the town I live in instead of from where I'm now assigned?"

"Let me check your records. I see you're a corporate lawyer. I also see you are assigned, looks like on average twenty cases a year. Guys in private practice in your town do at most one a year. Most do one every three years. You're overdue for a break. I'll assign you to your own town. There isn't much indigency there, so I don't suppose you'll be called upon very often. I'm sure you won't mind."

"Thank you, Your Honor. No, in truth, I won't miss it."

"I can't change what's already been assigned, but you'll get no new ones for a long time. Also, let me tell you Judge Freeman put a note in your record saying you're always prepared and a pleasure to have in his courtroom. Thought you might want to know."

"I'll remember to thank him when I see him next. Thank you, Your Honor."

And out of Dodge I went...on my own...unaccompanied by the court bailiff.

REALITY CHECK

(Tannenbaum does a TV deal)

This next story takes place many years after the ones I've related so far. By then, I had left my job as a corporate intellectual property lawyer and had become a partner in a law firm. Intellectual property law encompasses not only patents, but also trademarks and copyrights and includes, among other things, licenses with entertainment entities, such as sports and entertainment networks.

It was a warm Friday morning. The Friday before Labor Day weekend to be exact. I was looking forward to decompressing over a well-deserved long weekend. Lawyers for hire do not have nine-to-five jobs, and I had been going non-stop for several weeks with no end in sight.

"David?" It was the voice of a senior business partner on the other end of the phone line. "Would you mind joining me in conference room five? I have a matter that needs attention."

I suppose in the military the answer would be, "Yes, sir! Be right there, sir!" In my case, I said, "On my way." Same result. When the person at the top makes a request, the person on the bottom treats it as a command.

The senior partner intercepted me outside the conference room to give me the quick run-down before taking me in to meet with the parties waiting inside. The essence of the problem was that our firm's client had paid several million dollars to a man named Joe to develop, and bring to TV, a show called RealityCheck. The money was now gone and RealityCheck had yet to be produced. The firm's client had lost his millions.

Except now Joe was back. His latest gambit was to ask the client for another two million. The client's first response had been not just "no!" but "hell no!" But, as my partner explained, Joe had tentatively struck a three-party deal between 1) himself, 2) a well-known and very reliable TV producer called TV Productions (TVP for short), and 3) a major TV network, whereby the TV network would guarantee ten million dollars against future profits once the pilot was delivered. A deal too good for the firm client to pass up.

Everyone who heard about the deal said that it was too good to be true. Everyone, that is, except a vice-president of TVP, as well as TVP's in-house lawyer, who were in the conference room to finalize the relationship between Joe and TVP. They wore skeptical looks, which came through loud and clear.

Introductions were made around the table, but before any business could be transacted, the senior partner who had summoned me was called away on an emergent matter. Left behind was Joe; his friend Rosa McGee; TVP's vice president in charge of special projects, John Alexander; TVP's lawyer, Nancy Jenkins; and, of course, me. "So just why are you and Nancy here today?" I asked the vice president. "What do you want from our client?"

"First," the vice president said, "I wouldn't be wasting my time here today if the network deal wasn't solid. This is too good to let slip away, but we need to nail down exactly what is deliverable, time frames, percentages, you know, the usual details. And second, to be blunt about it, the pilot was mostly finished before we got involved, but it will require roughly two million more to complete. We only have a thirty-day window for delivery, so everything is compressed. We must have a firm commitment from your client and guarantees that the two mil will be deposited on time."

"Let me understand. You are asking for our client, who as I understand it, has already sunk millions into this project, to hand over another two million to Joe on the hope he'll complete the pilot in time. Do I have that right?"

"Not exactly," the lawyer Jenkins replied. "TVP will sign a contract with your client in which our company promises to supervise the completion of the pilot and guarantees that it be delivered on time. Surely you trust TVP. We're the gold standard."

I couldn't argue with the gold standard statement. TVP was highly respected in the industry. "What are the terms of that contract?"

Jenkins made a "duh" face. "That's what John Alexander and I are doing here today, of course. I'm going to ask John to outline the terms of the deal for you. That's what we'll be negotiating."

"Happy to do that," Alexander added, "but I need a few minutes with Joe first. Is there a room we can use?"

"You can use this room," I responded. "Ms. Jenkins and I and Ms. McGee will go across the hall. Come get us when you're ready. We'll be just across over there."

When we were seated in a small room across the hall, I handed Jenkins my business card and asked for hers. She reached in her bag and handed me a card engraved with the name of TV Productions and their local address. But her name was not on it.

"Oh," she apologized, "I'm in the process of relocating my office and my new cards aren't ready."

"I assume," I said, "it will be okay with you if I take control of drafting the contract."

"We have to sign it by Tuesday. If you can get it done by then it'll save me the trouble."

I pulled out my pen and legal pad. "While we're waiting for the business terms, which I assume will also include payment times and certifications, how about if you and I get the boring details out of the way."

"Such as?"

"Like the exact legal name of TV Productions, state of incorporation, jurisdiction, that stuff. New Jersey, New York or where? The typical boilerplate."

"Look it up!" Nancy barked. "Typical outside counsel! Adding irrelevant material just to run the bill up! Pull it off a computer and save your client money!"

"You have a preference for jurisdiction?" I said, surprised at her flare-up, but putting it down to being a negotiation tactic.

"Look, Tannenbaum, this contract won't ever be litigated. A handshake will do. But if you insist on making a phone book out of this deal, then be my guest! And use all the boilerplate you want, 'cause I won't be a party to such foolery!"

This was going to be one of those long days. And to think at the end of it I would get to spend the long weekend holed up in my home office working on the details. From what I had gathered, the client was pressing hard to make the deal and didn't want the lawyers to get in the way. Our client's two million dollars was apparently burning a hole in his pocket and he was pressing to deliver the money on Tuesday at the latest. TVP was pressing for an early money transfer as well, so all that stood in the way was the details.

Tuesday morning might have dawned bright and clear, but I had no clue how Tuesday morning actually dawned because I had been up most of the night finishing the contract. Finally pleased with the result, I had allowed myself two hours sleep just before daybreak. The contract was due on the senior partner's desk no later than nine a.m.

At seven forty-five, I stepped out of the shower and said to my wife, "Something's wrong."

"What's wrong? With what? The shower?"

"The deal I've been working on."

"I thought you said you had it all worked out."

"That's just it. The deal language is fine. Very good actually. But...I don't know. It's all wrong."

"How?"

"I don't know. Perhaps something the lawyer said. Perhaps something else. Something about the dynamics is off. I just don't know what it is."

"What are you going to do about it?"

"I don't know. It's not my deal. I'm only the scrivener on this one. And the details in the contract are solid. But still..."

"Lack of sleep can do that," my wife suggested.

"Perhaps."

At eight fifty, I approached the senior partner's office, still without a clue as to what was bothering me. "Tell him I have to see him the moment he comes in," I told his secretary when I found his office empty.

"He was in early today. I think he's in a conference room with someone. I'll tell him to call you when he's back."

I made my way back to my office, two floors below, wondering how much damage I was about to do to my credibility when I told a senior partner that something was wrong with a transaction his client was desperate to make, but unable to articulate anything other than, "Don't do it, but I have no idea why not."

The dreaded phone call finally came at nine thirty-five. Up I trudged, moving slower the closer I came to his large corner office. "Okay," he said, "I understand you wanted to see me. I need to tell you something as well. Why don't you go first?"

Why don't you go first and maybe I'll find a way to slip back to my office without destroying my reputation? "I don't know how to say this without sounding...well to put it bluntly, stupid."

"After the morning I've had, nothing can be too stupid. Out with it. We're on the clock."

"The contract is ready to sign. But...but it's my advice to instruct the client not to sign it because..."

"Because why?"

"Just because. That's all I can say. Something's wrong and before you ask all I can say is, I don't know. I know that sounds..."

"Hold up." His hands were in the air in front of him as if stopping a bull from charging. "I was in the conference room with Rosa McGee when you came in earlier. She called early today and told me just what you told me. Something was wrong with the deal. Only, unlike you, she knew what it was."

"What..."

"Rosa didn't like that lawyer Jenkins. Then it occurred to her that she had seen the lawyer on TV. In a commercial. And this morning, just now, she showed me pictures from a talent agency. Pictures proving that both the lawyer Nancy Jenkins, and John Alexander the vice president are actors. Apparently, they picked up business cards from the lobby of TV Productions."

"I'm sorry I didn't see through them on Friday," I said by way of apology.

"Don't beat yourself up. None of us did. Rosa feels worse because she exposed her friend Joe as a fraud. But, as she said, better now than after she married him." He then looked at me sheepishly. "I suppose I should have told you this up front," he began, "but…but I suppose I wanted to believe what the client told me. Joe just got out of prison. He served eighteen months for embezzlement, nothing to do with the client. Seems Joe convinced more than one client that prison, which I had not known about, had reformed him and to give him another chance. I guess that's what makes a con a con."

THE RICHARDSONS

(Check and Double Check)

Most of the work in house closings in New Jersey, at least back when I was doing them, was handled by the buyer's lawyer, usually in the buyer's lawyer's office. Since my office was inside a corporate building, I held what few closings I had in the office of the realtor. Back then, the lending bank would deliver the loan check to the closing lawyer for deposit in the lawyer's trust account. The check would be made payable to the lawyer, as well as to each of the borrowers. As with all checks, prior to deposit, the lawyer, as well as the borrowers, would endorse the back of the check. The endorsed mortgage check, together with any additional funds received from the buyer, would then be delivered to the lawyer's bank for deposit in the lawyer's trust account. Delivery to the bank could be in person, but usually was by mail.

At the closing, the lawyer would pay off all debts (real estate taxes then due, seller's mortgage, old water bills, unpaid judgments, etc.) by sending the lawyer's trust account check to the creditors. The balance after all debts were paid (the proceeds from the sale) belonged to the seller, and the lawyer then would deliver a trust account check for the proceeds to the seller.

Picture this: At the closing, the lawyer (me in this case) is writing checks on a trust account that won't have money in it until the mortgage loan check arrives at the bank and the check clears. The loan check will not even be mailed to the bank until after the closing. So unless there are other funds in the trust account, it could be two or more days until the trust account has enough money in it to cover all the checks being written at the closing. Be assured that I didn't dream up this prone-to-mischief procedure. I was just following standard practice.

The closing of the Richardson's new home went picture perfect. The sellers had my trust account check for approximately one hundred thousand dollars, and with big smiles on their faces left the closing, their car already packed for the drive to Florida and their new life. The buyers had equally large smiles as they headed out to their new home.

I dutifully filled out the bank deposit slip and slid it into the deposit envelope where I had previously already inserted the mortgage check. I then carefully sealed the envelope, checked that the proper postage was in place, and on my way back to my office dropped the deposit envelope into a convenient mailbox. All very nice and tidy.

The first problem surfaced an hour later. At least this one was easily solved.

"Hello, Mr. Tannenbaum," the pleasant voice on the other end said. "This is Cindy Dawson, head teller at First Federal Bank."

Head tellers don't call for social reasons, so I'm thinking that this is not good news. "Yes, Cindy, what can I do for you?"

"Mr. and Mrs. Sellers are here in the bank. They have a check drawn on your trust account for $102,406.87. Did you write that check?"

She was calling me, of course, because there was not enough money in the account to cover the check. Nor would there be for another two or three days—not until the bank received the check that, at that moment, was still lying at the bottom of a mailbox. "I did," I said, preparing to be scolded—or worse.

"I assume you had a house closing today?"

"Yes. The mortgage check to cover the Sellers's check is already in the mail. I even used one of the bank's pre-addressed envelopes."

"Okay. I'll make a note of that. We'll honor the trust check then. Sorry to bother you."

"Thank you, Cindy. Appreciate you checking with me."

Imagine a bank doing that today! By honoring the check, they had, in essence, made a one hundred thousand dollar loan to me with no collateral and with only my word that a check was in the mail.

But as I said, that was only problem one. Problem two came two days later, when Head Teller Dawson called me again.

"Sorry to bother you a second time, Mr. Tannenbaum," she began. "The envelope arrived this morning. I have it right in front of me. The deposit slip shows two checks, one for twenty thousand and some cents, and one for eighty-six thousand. I assume the eighty-six thousand is the mortgage check."

"That's right. The other one is a certified personal check from the buyers."

"Unfortunately, only the personal check is here. There's no mortgage check."

"I know for sure that I placed them both in the envelope."

"We'll keep looking then. In the meantime, I have to tell you that protocol requires the bank to assume that one of the bank employees has stolen the check, and unfortunately we're required to notify the FBI and the postal inspectors if this isn't straightened out by the close of business today."

What a mess, David. FBI. Postal Inspectors. Not to mention the state bar for overdrawing a trust account.

The file was in my home office. I called my wife and asked her to go through the file and search for the check. If it wasn't in the deposit envelope, I figured, then it must be in my file.

But it wasn't.

I asked my wife to look again, but it still wasn't.

I called the real estate office where we closed title, asking them search the closing room.

Nothing.

Search again, please?

Still nothing.

The bank president called. Same questions as before. Same answers as before, and same warning as before.

This was a full-pack-of-Tums day if ever there was one.

In desperation, I called the Richardsons, the folks who had bought the new house.

"We're all packed up ready to move tomorrow," the wife informed me. "My husband is out of town and I don't know where he put the files."

"Please call him and ask him to call me. Or give me his number, and I'll call him."

She gave me the number of the office where he was working. Thank goodness he answered the phone. I explained what I was looking for.

After a long silence he said, "You're talking about the eighty-six thousand dollar mortgage check, right?"

"Right."

"Well, I, um, slipped it out of your envelope, you know, the envelope you put it in after we all signed it. I just wanted to see it one last time. Never seen so much money in one place. I was signing my life away and just wanted to hold the check for a moment."

And then what?

"I put it back."

"In the deposit envelope?"

"Yes."

"You positive?"

"Pretty positive."

"Pretty positive" was not an encouraging answer. In fact, it was a downright chilling answer.

It was time to press him. By the morning, it would be the FBI inviting us both in for a visit.

"Any chance you did something else with it? Think hard about what you did with that check."

"Like what?"

I raised my eyes to the ceiling and took a deep breath. Like putting it in your pocket!!! "I don't know. Like putting it in your...own file."

"I suppose I could have. What with everything going on. Don't think so. But possible."

"Can you check?"

"I won't be home 'til late tonight."

"Call your wife and have her look. Late tonight is much too late."

"It's that important?"

On what planet wouldn't it be important? "Yes, it's that important."

I paced for an hour and twelve minutes, not knowing who would call first: His wife, the FBI, some postal guy, or the state bar. Only one of those calls would be welcome.

The phone rang, and nervously I picked it up, my blood pressure no doubt having reached stratospheric levels.

"I found it!" came the cheery voice of Mrs. Richardson. "The check was in his file. What should I do?"

"I need to have you drive it to my bank." For her, that would be a forty-five minute drive.

"I can do that. But won't they be closed?"

"Trust me. They'll be open for you. I'll call and let them know you're coming. Ask for Cindy, the head teller. She'll be expecting you."

I can't tell you how happy the bank was to learn that the check was on its way to them. Since protocol required them to assume that one of their employees had stolen it, the entire bank building had been in lockdown all day. Customers were being escorted in one at a time to transact business. All trash was being dumped onto a basement floor and carefully searched. All desk drawers had likewise been gone through. In short, they were in full catch-a-thief mode.

I had reached the bank exactly eight minutes short of their notifying the Feds. "Then the real fun would have begun," the bank president said when he called back to thank me for finding the missing check. "Dealing with the regulatory mess and the bank auditors would have been a total nightmare."

Truth be told, I was much more relieved to have avoided my own nightmare.

Judge with a Heart

(Or Show Me Your Cash)

Judge Freeman, the municipal judge whose court I was assigned to for pro bono work (before Judge Hildebrand transferred me) announced his retirement on the day when I next appeared before him. I have to assume that my appearance in his courtroom was not a factor in his decision to step down from the bench. But I wasn't about to explore that possibility with him. Sleeping tigers and all that.

While waiting for my matter to be heard, I sat through several other cases. One was noteworthy, not so much for its outcome, but for understanding how nothing is ever as straightforward as it first seems.

Two men, apparently in their mid-sixties and representing themselves in court, had been arrested for sleeping in an abandoned building. The arresting officer proceeded to tell the judge how on January 15th at two in the morning he found Able and Baker in the building sound asleep under a pile of cardboard boxes.

"How do you plead?" the judge asked the men.

"What's that, Judge?"

"Well, did you do it or not? Were you in that building on that night? Yes or no?"

"We's in some building."

"I'll take that as a guilty plea."

"Does that mean we'll have to pay money?"

"Why were you in the building?"

"Sleeping."

"I know you were sleeping. But why in that building? I happen to know that that building is marked with a no trespassing sign. Why not sleep in the park?"

"Cold, Judge. Real cold it was. Cops did chase us from the park early on and told us to go someplace warm."

Judge Freeman turned to the officer. "How cold was it that night?"

The officer consulted his notes. "Plenty cold. I believe it was something like five below."

"Oh, that must have been when we had that cold snap. I remember. So why did you arrest them? I thought you allowed them to come indoors when the weather was bad?"

"We did, Your Honor. But ever since the fire we're under orders to keep them out of the abandoned buildings. As you said, that building had a no trespassing sign on it. It was on fire just a week before."

"But if they slept out in the open in that cold they'd freeze to death."

"Two did, Your Honor. That night two did die. We didn't find them in time."

"That's my point. We can't leave them out in the cold. Now you're telling me the mayor won't allow them inside either."

"I'm just following orders, sir. When they go inside, they light fires. The places burn down."

"It's a tough problem, I know. Here's a new order. Any time it's too cold outside and you find these folks where they shouldn't be, just bring them to the jail. Let them sleep inside.

What good does it do to give them tickets for sleeping in a building when they will die outside? They have no money to pay for a motel room or whatever. And they have nowhere to go."

The officer shrugged as if to say this was far above his pay grade.

"Okay," Judge Freeman said. "I'll fine you each five dollars. And next time you're cold out there come over to the jail and we'll let you sleep inside for free."

"Even if we're drun...we got us some whiskey in us?"

"Whiskey and all. You come over to the jail to stay warm."

"We won't be arrested?"

"You won't be arrested."

"We can go in the morning?"

"You'll be free to leave in the morning."

To the courtroom in general Judge Freeman said, "I don't know how this will get paid for. But I do know it's not right to allow anyone to die of the cold." To Able, he said, "What are you doing?"

"Searching for my money. I know I has one dollar. Maybe even more."

"That's a quarter you have there. Not a dollar."

"I have two more of these," Able said, proudly opening his hand to show off his three quarters.

"Is that all you have?"

"Maybe a dollar somewheres. And I was hopin' to save somethin' for a drink. Mouth's awful dry."

"Okay. Your fine is a quarter. Pay the clerk on the way out."

Whereupon Able turns and starts for the door, a big grin on his face because he now has enough money left for a drink.

Whereupon Baker walks toward the Judge. "What about me, Judge? I have some money too. What's my..."

"Come on Baker," Able calls, his hand locked onto Baker's filthy T-shirt. "Let's get out of here before we don't have enough for a drink."

"But I want to pay my..."

"Do you have a quarter?" Judge Freeman says to Baker. When Baker nods, the judge says, "Your fine is a quarter as well. Now get out of here and stay out of trouble."

"I be tryin', Judge. I be tryin'. Ain't easy."

"Come on, Baker," Able says, tugging even harder. "You keep talkin', judge'll take all our money. Now let's git."

Freeman called my case next. I plead my client guilty to public drunkenness and ask for a suspended sentence provided my client goes into rehab. The judge agreed, saying, "This is his third rehab. Let's hope this one works. The others certainly didn't."

"Appreciate that, Your Honor. And, by the way, thanks for the nice comments in my file."

"You heard me say I'm leaving the bench. Been serving here for going on twenty years. I thought I could do some good. But I don't know now. It's time someone with a fresh mind takes over. What do you do with folks like Able and Baker? I can't stop them from drinking. Heck, I can barely keep them alive. No, this wears a person out. Thank you for your service."

I was thankful for Judge Hildebrand's transfer, but I felt like a rat leaving a sinking ship nonetheless. I'm not sure why, given that some new judge would be taking the place of Judge Freeman. However, that feeling quickly dissipated when I got back to my office and realized I wouldn't have to defended any more folks who ran over a police officer, or cut a policeman's arm, or ran a red light while intoxicated.

But somehow I still felt guilty.

Dr. Sam Takes A Dream Vacation

(Which Turns Into a Nightmare)

This story begins idyllically enough when Dr. Sam and his wife, Janet, set off for a sun-filled vacation in a Caribbean island country, which I'll call Jamaica. The vacation package included six nights at a beach resort, airfare out of Philadelphia, airport transfers, and a myriad of other goodies and activities at the resort. The TV advertisement featured a romantic horseback ride along a white sand beach illuminated by a full moon. What could be bad about that?

In fact, it was all perfect. Until it wasn't. As it turns out, the horses were high-strung retired racehorses that tended to speed off at top speed when excited or agitated. Doc's horse got spooked at a certain point and took off like a shot. And apparently not wanting to be slowed by a rider, the horse bucked wildly and then stopped suddenly. Doc went flying over the horse's head and landed in the sand in front of the now galloping pack. All but one of the horses missed trampling him. But the one that caught him did a job on his face and head. When the sand cleared, Janet found her husband unconscious with a shallow pulse and his head all but flattened. But for the relatively forgiving sand, Doc would have died instantly.

It took two hours to transport him to the local hospital where the emergency doctor pronounced Doc too far gone to spend time or effort trying to save him. They refused to put him in a room, instead wheeling him to the end of a corridor to await his turn to enter heaven, or wherever Doc's destiny would take him.

Janet had other thoughts. She called a private jet medical transport company to, as she later said to me, "retrieve my husband from that hellhole and take him to Miami where he'd be treated by real doctors."

"We can be in Jamaica in two hours," the jet company informed her, "after ten thousand dollars is deposited in our account."

"It's ten o'clock in the evening where I live! And it's Saturday!" Janet exclaimed. "How the ----- am I supposed to transfer money at this time of day?"

"Sorry, I'm not authorized to change corporate policy."

Janet called her bank back home hoping to at least hear a recording with an emergency number. It was a tiny one-branch bank and the president of the bank happened to be in his office and he himself answered the phone. Janet actually knew the man and, upon hearing what had happened to Doc, he called the transport company and guaranteed the funds would be transferred on Monday.

What Janet didn't know was that the transport company had already dispatched a plane to Jamaica from a neighboring island and the medical crew was actually due at the hospital within a half-hour.

A week to stabilize Doc's diabetes and he was ready for the first of three major reconstructive surgeries. Five months later, his eye sockets having been rebuilt along with his right jaw and cheek structure, Doc was ready to resume his medical practice. Short-term memory was an issue, but Janet and Doc were told it would slowly improve.

Total cost of treatment: A quarter million dollars.

The resort refused to even acknowledge that Doc had been injured at their place, let alone cover any portion of the medical bills. Nor did they respond to Janet's request to tell her who their liability insurance carrier was. Not a woman to be scorned, Janet thereupon established a routine of driving to the Philadelphia airport and passing out flyers to people boarding the plane to Jamaica. (This was at a time before security measures restricted non-passengers from entering the gate area.) The flyers simply had printed on them the name of the resort and the words: ASK THEM WHAT HAPPENED TO DOC AND WHY THEY WON'T PAY DOC'S MEDICAL BILLS.

Weeks turned into months with no change in attitude on the part the resort. That's when Janet contacted me about legal recourse. Doc and Janet were long-time friends of mine, and I had been closely following Doc's medical recovery, but I was only vaguely aware of Janet's weekly Philadelphia expedition. Apparently she had ruffled a few feathers, because at one point the city required her to obtain a parade permit, which she dutifully did. Philadelphia kept adding to the parade permit requirements and Janet continued to match them move for move.

Finally, she had enough. "I want you to file suit!" she insisted. "Those SOB's destroyed my husband and won't give us a dime! They're pressuring Philadelphia to stop me and it's getting to the point where I'll be arrested if I continue. I have no idea how much our medical insurance is actually going to cover, but medical bills are only a small part of what this has cost us anyway. Doc's medical practice has pretty much evaporated!"

"But we're in New Jersey," I said. "You have to sue on the island. I can't..."

"Find a way! It's not right!"

In fact, there was a way. A New Jersey court had recently ruled that a New Jersey resident could sue an out-of-state defendant in New Jersey if an accident caused by the defendant's negligence befell that resident and the negligent party had enticed the injured party to visit the out-of-state location.

Advertising in New Jersey for a romantic week in the sun was most certainly intended to entice New Jersey residents to the Jamaican resort. And putting resort guests on an easily-spooked excitable horse provided the basis for an assertion of negligence.

Doc's case fit both elements, so we were able to file suit. But the resort needed to be "served" with the appropriate legal papers which, in the case of a major lawsuit like this one, cannot be done by simply dropping the papers in the mail. And because Jamaica is a foreign country, the requirements of service are more complicated than simply hiring a process server to show up at the resort.

It turns out there is a complicated, but doable, scheme for serving foreign defendants. In essence, service is achieved through a process involving the U. S. State Department and the foreign government's liaison office. All via some treaty or another. It took about six weeks, but eventually the Resort In The Sun was duly and properly served.

The clock was now ticking. The resort had two months to file what's called an "answer" in the Newark, New Jersey, federal court, where we had filed suit. That meant that the resort would have to hire a stateside attorney, and Doc and Janet would finally have someone to negotiate with. At least that was the hope.

On the last day for the resort to respond to the suit I received a phone call from a Mr. Sommers who identified himself as an insurance negotiator. He said he was currently in

Europe settling a matter but would "swing by" the States on his way back to the Caribbean to talk with me about what he referred to as Doc's "meritless" case.

I agreed to file a paper with the court saying that we agreed to an extension of the time for the resort to file its answer.

But where to meet Sommers? Certainly not my corporate office. And even more certainly, not my living room. I thought of the public library. What about a diner? Yea, a good New Jersey Greek diner. (Are there any other kind in Jersey?)

Sanity took hold. I called a friend who was a partner in one of the state's largest law firms. The firm had just moved into new digs in a very modern office tower and hadn't spared any expense. Beyond lavish is the only way to describe the space.

"I didn't know you were associated with this firm," Sommers commented, as he settled into a plush chair in the beautifully appointed conference room a week later. He said he had just flown all night into Newark from London and was "a bit knackered".

"I'm not affiliated with this firm," I advised him, "but they'll be lead counsel when this comes to trial."

"Oh, I see," Sommers responded, clearly not happy at that prospect. Apparently he had researched me, saw that I wasn't a personal injury attorney and assumed that his experienced trial lawyers would be able to wrap a patent lawyer like me around their little fingers.

"What's 'oh, I see' mean?" I asked.

Sommers ignored the question. "Even assuming you could obtain a judgment here in the States," he said, "what's it worth? The Jamaican government will never allow currency to leave the island. Of course you're aware that the island has strict currency control."

I actually knew nothing about currency controls and had

no idea how currency controls even worked. But I did what I always do when I'm at a loss. I bluffed. "Not a big deal," I replied.

"You're not making sense. You'll never get your money off the island."

"I bet the resort has assets on other islands. Maybe even in the States. And, by the way, have you considered a doctor's earning capacity over a lifetime? Many, many millions. That's what we'll get. If the hotel doesn't pay up, I bet I can get the court to block advertising in the States. There'll be no more planeloads of people flying to your beautiful island from up here. And that's..."

"Enough of your fancy bluff. Here's the deal. You are right about one thing. If this case were tried in the U.S., the verdict could be multi-millions. But this resort is independently owned, and its only assets are in Jamaica. And because of the currency controls, you'll never get so much as a hundred dollars off the island.

Of course, if you settle with the insurance company, then you won't have to try to enforce a court judgment. The insurance company will be the one paying, and the money will be coming from London, so no currency control issues.

"And so what are you offering?"

"I was authorized to settle the matter in Europe for five million U.S. dollars. I managed to come in a wee bit under that. The insurance company won't fuss if the amount I didn't spend in Europe goes to your client. Otherwise..."

"And just what is that 'wee bit' amount?"

"Two hundred thousand."

"Even just Doc's medical bills are higher than that."

"Three hundred."

"Five million."

"Five million is all I was authorized to spend. Total. I told you I had to settle the matter in Europe. All I can pay is what I have left over."

"Tell me the real left over amount, then."

"Seven hundred thousand."

"Make it a million and I'll ask my client. But my advice to them will be not to settle for less than five million."

"You're not listening. I only have seven hundred. Not a penny more."

"That's left over money from some other matter and has nothing to do with Doc. Five million."

"Seven hundred. Take it or leave it."

"As you well know, it's up to the client. And, for the record, I'm not buying this currency limitation thing."

"That's the best I can do."

"If you wait here, I'll call them. But I'm recommending they not accept."

"Take it!" Janet said immediately when I got her on the line. "Doc's had enough and wants to end this now."

It's only a first offer. I believe we can get..."

"Take it! Take the seven hundred thousand! Even the thought of going to trial is too much for Doc to contemplate, let alone actually going through it. He's adamant. No more negotiating."

"But the medical bills. The loss of inc..."

"Finally got it all covered by insurance. Take the offer."

"Okay," I mumbled, not happy with their decision. But that was my problem, not theirs. Janet couldn't have been any clearer, and Doc came on the line to confirm that he wanted what Janet had said.

"They accepted your offer," I told Sommers a few moments later. Then, on a whim, I added, "but with an additional condition. You said the government does not allow money to leave the island."

"That's correct," Sommers asserted. "Their currency control is incredibly strict."

"So what about an additional million dollars to be used only on the island? Certainly, the government can't be opposed to money being spent locally."

"What?"

"Look, this is a multimillion dollar case. You said so yourself. Paying less than two million is a good deal. I'm thinking that between the insurance company and the resort, there's a lot more settlement money to be had than seven hundred thousand. Tell me I'm wrong."

"So let me understand. Your client accepts seven hundred thousand dollars paid into your attorney trust account as long as they get an additional million dollars deposited to an account on the island which, because of the currency controls, can only be spent on the island. Do I have that right?"

"Exactly."

"Show me to a telephone and I'll enquire."

Sommers was back in less than fifteen minutes. "We're rounding up to an even million," he announced. Nine hundred will be deposited in your account and the additional one hundred will go into a bank account you will open on the island, with the proviso that the money in that account will be spent only on the island. Buy a condo, donate it, or whatever."

"You have a deal," I said, extending my hand.

"You got what?" Janet exclaimed when I told her about the additional three hundred thousand. "That's astounding, but Doc will never go back there to claim the other hundred. He can't even bear to hear the name of the island said out loud."

"I have some ideas about that money," I said. "But one thing at time."

A week later a gentleman from a bank in Jamaica called me to get the information necessary to set up an account to hold the $100,000 that had, in fact, already been sent to the bank, per my agreement with Sommers. Playing dumb, I asked the banker what would be the easiest way to get the funds transferred to my U.S. account. Write myself a check? Request a wire transfer?

But that was not to be. The banker confirmed what Sommers had told me about currency controls. "The island government forbids currency transfer of any form without direct approval from the Minister of Finance," the banker told me. "But you can spend the money on the island any way you want."

"Supposing I were to come down to Jamaica, withdraw the money and fly back with it in my suitcase?"

"When you leave you have to declare how much money you are taking out, which cannot be more than how much you declared you were bringing in when you arrived."

"And if I happen to write down the wrong amounts 'by mistake'?"

"Such a mistake is not advised. Jamaica does not hesitate to jail people who attempt to violate their Currency Control Act.

"Oh. And one other thing," he added. I've been instructed that the money in this account falls under the jurisdiction of Mr. Jamison Clarke, Minister of Finance. Only he personally can authorize withdrawals from that account."

"What? Why? What the hell is going on?"

"I wish I knew more. Sorry."

I hang up and dialed the Ministry of Finance, only to have

the banker's statement completely confirmed. I asked to speak to Mr. Clarke directly but was told that Minister Clarke will only speak to people face-to-face. No telephone. In person. By appointment only."

"But..."

"If that is all, sir, I will say goodbye now."

The phone went dead.

"So?" Janet said when I informed her of these latest developments. "Go on down to the island and have a great vacation. Buy yourself a condo or something nice. We don't care what you do. We never asked for that money, so do with it what you want."

Sounded like a good idea to me. I called Minister Clarke's office back and got on his calendar for a Tuesday in the upcoming month.

A couple of new bathing suits, a ton of sun block and my wife and I were all set for our own adventure in idyllic Jamaica.

Stay tuned.

Even the Mighty Sometimes Apologize

(But Not Often)

When you walk the halls of certain law firms, the names on the doors read like a political who's who, with a former secretary of state in one corner and former vice-president or attorney general in the opposite corner. This is the realm of folk who are accustomed to achieving what they set out to achieve. And Heaven help anyone who gets in their way.

Unfortunately for them, however, the law firm on the opposite side of any negotiating table usually has the same kind of office lineup. In a sense, the only difference is the names on the doors. They, too, are accustomed to working their collective wills.

Despite such a seemingly irreconcilable face-off, clients hire lawyers to get deals negotiated and signed. So even though everyone in the room wants their own way, compromise is necessary. But giving in doesn't come easy to these folks, and bickering over often insignificant issues is almost de rigeur.

So, imagine legal negotiations between two major corporations that have been going on for close to three months. This following eight months of business discussions. One corporation is to manufacture a machine that will be branded and distributed by the other. An example of such an arrangement (not the one I am discussing) would be Whirlpool manufacturing a refrigerator that will bear the name of, and be sold by, Maytag. Screw-ups by one company can easily do major harm to the other company. Thus every mundane detail must be discussed, beat to death, compromised on, written down, re-discussed, re-resolved and re-written down until the clients (mind you, not the lawyers) have had enough and decide to move forward or end the discussions.

In our scenario, the time for discussion and argument was quickly drawing to an end. In five hours, at three o'clock in the afternoon, the board of the company whose name will appear on the product (by far the more prestigious company of the two) is set to meet to either approve or reject the deal. For various reasons, this is a hard deadline, and it's a one-bite-at-the-apple situation. Either both parties will sign by three p.m., or the deal is off. Permanently off.

A limo is parked at the curb forty-three stories below the offices of the manufacturing corporation's law firm, where the final provisions of the deal are still being argued over. It is a one-hour drive to where the board will be meeting, but the general counsel has demanded an hour to be briefed on the terms of the deal so he, in turn, can brief the board. In essence, then, the limo must pull away from the curb within the next three hours.

I, as a junior lawyer working for the law firm representing the prestigious company, finding myself with nothing remaining to argue over, say to a junior lawyer for the other side, "Who's going to be signing the contract on your side?

Assuming, that is, that the rest of your team will stop nit-picking long enough that the contract can be signed."

"I assume it will be Smith over there," he answers, pointing to a tall thin man in heated discussion with his counterpart on the other side.

"Is Mr. Smith an officer of your client?"

"Not that I know of, but he's the chief negotiator and has the full backing of the chairman."

"Well, then, who exactly is he?"

"He's a hired consultant. The chairman has used him for many deals. He has full authority."

"I have never seen a contract signed by someone called 'Chief Negotiator'. Better buck it upstairs, so we get the names right on the signature line."

"Your point being...?"

"This contract is worth well over five hundred million dollars if it plays out to term. Maybe even more. That's why it's going to our client's full board, and if they approve, it'll be our chairman signing it."

"What's so wrong with Smith signing for our side?"

"I can't imagine our general counsel even presenting it to our board unless your client, actually your chairman, has already signed it."

"Smith will sign for our chairman. If it makes you happy, he'll even sign the chairman's name."

I couldn't believe what I was hearing. "But Smith's not an officer of your client and apparently has no written authority to sign on your chairman's behalf either. We'll need an officer. I strongly urge you to get moving on this."

Negotiations continued, the give-and-take on the last several points proceeding slowly. Leaving the tough stuff for last has its advantages—and its disadvantages."

"Two hours to wheels rolling," someone announced.

"So have you resolved who will be signing for your client?" I asked again a while later.

"I told you," my counterpart snapped, "Smith, the chief negotiator."

"And I told you that you had better escalate and get an officer to sign because otherwise this deal just may not happen," I snapped back.

"I did escalate. To the partner in charge of the client account and he agrees with me."

"I believe we'll be demanding a letter of authority from your client giving Mr. Smith the authority to bind your client."

"The question of Smith's authority to sign is not your business!"

"It is my business if you expect us to tell our client it's okay for our chairman to sign this contract."

A few moments later the chief negotiator for our side— call him Jones—stormed over and called me aside. "I'm told you've been causing trouble over the signatures. Mr. Smith and I have been at this for months. Don't screw it all up now with legal mumbo jumbo. Of course he has authority to bind his side! He's negotiated all the terms and conditions and if he doesn't have authority then all we've done is a waste!"

"Unless he has proper written authority, he can't bind them. It's not my mumbo jumbo. It's the law. If it suits their needs downstream, Mr. Smith's company could simply walk away from the deal, claiming that the contract was never signed from their side by anyone authorized to do so."

"This is stupid!" Jones barked, glancing at his watch and

realizing he only had thirty more minutes to get everything wrapped up, get the contract put into final form, signed by the other side, and ready to present to his board. Looking directly at a lawyer from the other side, he demanded, "Get me your senior partner! We need to get to the bottom of this now!"

It took another ten minutes before a man wearing a perfectly formed bow tie framed by a highly starched collar appeared in the doorway. Before anyone could say anything, he said, "Let me assure everyone in this room that Mr. Smith has been granted full authority to sign on behalf of our client."

Jones turned to me and demanded, "Is that good enough for you, son?"

"Only if I can see written authority," I said, holding my ground.

"Young man!" Bow Tie snarled. "Are you questioning my veracity?"

"No, sir," I replied deciding to take a different approach. "What title should we put after Mr. Smith's name on the contract?"

Bow Tie turned to one of his own lawyers. "What position does Mr. Smith hold with the client?"

"He's not an employee, sir. He was hired to negotiate this matter."

"Oh." Bow Tie turned on his heel and disappeared.

Ten minutes to wheels rolling and another white-haired, bow-tied man enters the room. "I'm William Bentcraft, the senior managing partner," he announced in a perfectly manicured voice. "I am told that there is a question here of Mr. Smith's authority to sign a contract. Let me assure you that we have seen such authority."

"Could you please produce a copy..."

"I'm afraid it's been misplaced, but Mr. Smith does have

authority and he will sign the chairman's name under that authority."

"But..."

Jones, my client, glared at me. "The head of this firm says there is authority. That's good enough for me. Now get that contract signed and bring it down to the car. You have five minutes max!"

Knowing what would happen when the contract was presented to the general counsel I held my ground. "The first question you'll be asked by the general counsel when you brief him will be who signed the contract."

"That's my problem, not yours!"

"If this deal goes south, it'll be everyone's problem." I paused, took a deep breath, turned to the managing partner and said. "Sir, you do recognize that this contract is easily in the five hundred million dollar range? Possibly even higher. If your client were to deny that Smith had authority to bind them, your firm will be on the hook. Being able to produce a paper granting Mr. Smith authority to bind your client might just become more valuable to you than to my client."

"Who do you think you are lecturing, young man? If you worked for this firm I'd have you terminated!"

"That's enough!" barked Jones. "Get the contract signed and downstairs to me immediately!" With that, Jones marched straight to the elevator.

At two forty-five I was back in my office when I received a phone call.

CALLER: This is William Bentcraft. We met earlier here at my law firm.

ME: Yes, I recall we did.

BENTCRAFT: I owe you a major apology and I'm very embarrassed having to make this call in light of my uncalled-for behavior. But I need to request a big favor. Our firm never did receive a written authorization to allow Mr. Smith to bind our client. But I give you my word that I have now spoken to my client's chairman and he assured me that he will personally sign the contract later today. He can't sign now because he's out of his office."

ME: Isn't this between you and my client's general counsel? I don't understand why you're calling me."

BENTCRAFT: Your general counsel called our law firm requesting a copy of the document authorizing Mr. Smith to sign on behalf of the chairman. But, as I said, we don't have it. In fact, I've come to learn, contrary to what I was told, that it never existed. Your general counsel informed me that the contract will not be presented to your client's board unless I satisfy you that my client has personally agreed to all the terms and that there are no conditions yet to be fulfilled.

ME: And?"

BRENTCRAFT: And as I said, I personally spoke to the chairman and I have his assurance that he will deliver a fac-simile of his signature later today and a fully executed copy later in the week.

ME: I'm willing to accept your assurances, given the large liability, not to mention the reputational harm, your firm would suffer if it turns out you have no such assurance from your client.

BENTCRAFT: I very much appreciate your accepting my word as a gentleman. Now if you will please call your gener-al counsel, he is waiting for your go-ahead. We have...uh... one minute.

ME: Apology accepted. I'll make the call. To this day I have no idea if the general counsel used me as an intermedi-ary at this final stage because he didn't have time to run all the traps—or because it was his way to humble the mighty.

POST SCRIPT

During the life of the contract, over a billion dollars in revenue was generated, all of it based on what could be characterized as a telephonic handshake.

DIVORCE

(Nun style)

The law can be confusing at times—even to lawyers.

Witness Betty, a woman of about fifty, who timidly sat across from my desk and told me a story that was difficult for her to discuss, yet the circumstances required her to bare her soul. Betty is Catholic and was determined to become a nun.

Betty told me that there was a major impediment to her becoming a nun. She had been married.

"I thought celibacy was only going forward," I commented, knowing I was on shaky ground.

"Not for the order I will be joining. I need you to erase the marriage. They simply won't allow me in if I've been married."

"You can't erase a marriage," I replied.

"What if it was never consummated?"

"But you said you were living with your husband for five years. Now you say you never..."

"No never!"

Have you discussed this with a priest?"

"He referred me to the bishop. The bishop says if we lived as a married couple then I was married. But if the marriage is erased—he said 'annulled'—if my marriage is annulled by the civil courts then he can issue an annulment in the Catholic Church. With the annulment the order will accept me."

"I see. What have you done so far?"

"I went to see a lawyer. He said the fact that the marriage was never consummated is unimportant because we were married under common law in Pennsylvania, and a New Jersey judge cannot end a common law marriage."

"Did that lawyer tell you why a judge can't end a common law marriage?"

"He said something about I couldn't prove I was ever married."

"If the lawyer said you were never married, and you never consummated the marriage, then why not just tell the order you were never married?"

"But I believed I was married. I can't lie."

The law certainly created a catch-22 for Betty. She attempted to be married in a common law state. One of the elements of a divorce is to prove the marriage, or in the case of an annulment, to prove that a putative marriage was never consummated. There was no marriage certificate, no marriage license, no priest, no magistrate, nothing to show a marriage. Being somewhat of an expert on common law marriages from the Billy Bob matter, I thought otherwise. All I needed to do was provide a witness who could attest to the fact that they both got their mail at the same Pennsylvania residence and to testify that Betty's clothes, as well as her husband's clothes, were permanently in the Pennsylvania house and that they introduced each other as husband and wife and then we could prove the marriage so she'd get her annulment. Betty told me she had a friend who knew her when she was "married" and the friend had come to the house often.

We were ready to take on the court. Or so I thought.

Flash forward several months to a New Jersey courtroom and a grey-haired judge.

COURT CLERK: In the annulment matter of Betty Doe. Are the parties ready?

ME: We are.

JUDGE (before I could even walk through the gate separating the spectators from the participants): Counselor, I see nothing in your pleadings that proves a marriage. Without such proof I am afraid this court has no jurisdiction. You are wasting my time.

ME: Your honor, Betty was married under the common law of the Commonwealth of Pennsylvania and I have a witness who can provide proof...

JUDGE: You mean to tell me you plan to call your client to the stand to testify in open court that she lived in the same house with a man as husband and wife without benefit of a marriage license? I won't allow it.

ME: It's a fact, Your Honor. She believed she was married.

JUDGE: Frankly, I don't care what she believed or believes. If you have no marriage license then you have no marriage. If you have no marriage I certainly can't annul what never happened.

ME: But Your Honor, I...

JUDGE: Case dismissed.

ME: Your Honor. Please hear me out.

JUDGE: You have one minute. But I can't imagine what you can say to change the simple fact that you cannot prove a marriage—or even an attempt at a marriage. And I won't allow your client to talk about her...her sinful ways in open court.

ME: We are asking for an annulment. An annulment, as you well know, means that the marriage never existed. If there was no marriage before we came in here today then if you grant the annulment there will be no marriage when we leave. So no harm is done.

JUDGE: That logic works both ways. If there was no marriage before your client entered this court then your client doesn't require a note from me saying so. And there will be no marriage when she leaves.

ME: Your Honor, my client believes she entered into a marriage arrangement. She's come to you for help because there isn't any other place for her to go. If a judge can't fix her situation then who can? I told her that's what judges do, fix problems. We are asking for you to give full faith and credit to Pennsylvania law. Nothing more.

JUDGE: Mr. Tannenbaum, I would fix it if I could. I read your brief, but frankly I know nothing about common law marriages. You say Pennsylvania has such a thing, but I have no way of knowing that. More important, if they do have common law marriage I have no idea what is required to prove such a marriage.

ME: Your Honor, if you will allow us to postpone this hearing we can provide whatever type of proof of common law marriage you require.

JUDGE: I'm not saying I agree with you. But I will grant the postponement. If I do decide to rule, I'll want a legal memo from a member of the Pennsylvania Bar. You're right in one aspect. I'm here to help people and I will give full faith and credit to the law of another state. But I must tell you, I asked around, and no judge in this county recalls any divorce ever being granted based on a common law marriage. Annulment would fall in that category.

ME: Thank you, Your Honor. For the record, I also found no instances where a divorce was granted by this court based on a common law marriage. But I believe it's because it's so easy to just walk away from such a marriage since there is no record of it's ever having taken place. And that, in and of itself, is wrong. My client is trying to do the right thing here, and we appreciate your help.

JUDGE: You have one month. Clerk, set the date for re-hearing one month out. Good luck, Counselor.

* * *

I dusted off the Billy Bob memo, called my cousin Carl who is a Philadelphia lawyer, and asked him to review the memo, make any changes he deemed necessary, and send the memo back to me on his letterhead. Careful lawyer that my cousin is, he assigned a law clerk to research the law, and ten days later I received a work of art. My page-and-a-half had blossomed into a solid ten pages, complete with footnotes and citations. The memo had been signed by my cousin as well as two other lawyers, all of whom were members of the Pennsylvania bar. Attached to the memo were certifications of the good standing of each of the lawyers. I promptly filed the document with the court.

The hearing went as follows:

ME: If it please...

JUDGE: Mr. Tannenbaum, I accept the fact, based on the excellent memo you supplied in this matter, that Pennsylvania allows common law marriage. But as you well know, an essential element is absent in this case, namely, consummation. So, in fact there is no marriage and we are back where we started from I'm afraid.

ME: Thank you for considering the memo, Your Honor. In answer to your concern, I must note that New Jersey courts routinely grant annulments for New Jersey-based marriages where the facts show no consummation. I believe in those situations jurisdiction is predicated on the outward appearance of a valid marriage, the license, and the ceremony. Consummation is never really known and is always a fact to be determined once basic jurisdiction is achieved. So all we are asking at this point is to treat the Pennsylvania marriage the same as you would treat a New Jersey marriage. All the public elements are present but the private element of consummation is missing. We are asking you to hear testimony to that fact, make a determination, and if you find no consummation then declare the marriage void. Justice will then be done.

JUDGE: You may proceed, Counselor. Please put your client on the stand. She'll have to now testify in open court. You have instructed her as to that fact, no doubt.

ME: I have, Your Honor. And she is willing to so testify.

JUDGE: You may proceed.

ME: Thank you, Your Honor.

Betty then took the stand, told her story of how her wedding night went and, in response to my questions, testified as to her and her husband's clothes both being in the same house, how their mail was addressed, and a few other facts. Tears streamed down her face as she slowly walked back to her seat.

I then called her friend to the stand to corroborate Betty's story.

The judge studied his notes for an eternity before ultimately granting the annulment.

Looking back now on that day in the courtroom, I'm still not sure if Betty's wet face was from tears of regret or tears of shame. Or perhaps she was crying out of joyfulness that she was now one step closer to becoming a nun.

AUDI

(Drug Dealer Special)

This is mostly just a personal story, but it does have a legal angle.

I was thinking of buying an Audi just before the car became known for what was claimed to be unintended acceleration when the brakes were applied. It had also been reported that in some situations the brakes simply failed to work. I actually didn't know anything about that at the time I began looking for a used model. Why I wanted an Audi I can't recall, but I did.

This was at a time when a person wanting a used car pored through the classified ads in one or more newspapers. After a few weeks of looking at every used Audi classified ad I could find, I was pretty sure I knew the value of the car on a year-by-year basis. The model and year I was looking for was selling at between four and seven thousand dollars. I had seen two of the four thousand dollar cars and they were in terrible condition. I wanted something in good shape and was prepared to pay in the six-thousand-dollar range.

"Hey, look at this!" I exclaimed one Saturday night around midnight. My wife and I had been out to a party and had picked up the New York Times on the way home.

"I'll look at whatever it is in the morning," came the groggy reply.

"No. Here's an Audi, right year, good condition, for three thousand."

"You planning on calling them now? At midnight? Go to bed. It can wait until morning."

It was about 8:15 a.m. when I called. I knew it was a Sunday, and I knew it was rude to call so early. But they were the ones who placed the ad in the newspaper. They were the ones who wanted to sell a car. Or so my rationale went.

"You're the first to call," a man with a sleepy voice, said. "I suppose you want to see the car," he mumbled, not all that happy about being woken up.

I explained my situation and confirmed the price and the condition of the car. I told him I would leave my house within a half-hour.

"Won't hold it later than noon. Better hurry."

The car was in New York City—a more-than-two-hour drive from my home in New Jersey. We arrived at 11:40, parking in front of the house bearing the address he had given me. Five other cars were lined up ahead of us.

"It's my wife's car," the sleepy-voiced man said when he answered the door. "I think she put the wrong price on it 'cause the phone's been ringing all morning. But I told those other folks out there that some guy from Jersey called first, so it's yours if you want it."

"Mind if I..."

He thrust the keys into my hand even before I could get the question out.

This guy's in a hurry. Wonder what the problem is?

No problem, actually, from what I could tell. The car looked new, smelled new, drove new. Under the hood it looked new, not a grease smudge anywhere. Odometer read 3675 miles, and yes, the odometer was working. Not like a car I had bought as a teenager where the odometer had been disconnected for a hundred thousand miles before it was reconnected and sold to the first sucker (me) through the door.

"Well?" the man asked when I handed back the keys. "You buyin' it or should I pass the keys along to that guy over there?"

"Tell me the history. This is New York. The plates are from Florida. What's the story?"

"You want the car or not?"

"Yes, I want it. But why Florida plates?"

"Hey, which one of you was next?" the guy yelled over my shoulder.

"Johnny, what's the commotion?" A grey-haired woman had stepped out onto the porch where we were standing.

"You wanna deal with this, here!" the man snapped, slapping the keys into her hand and disappearing into the house.

"Don't know what's eatin' him these days. So where are we?"

"I was just asking why the car has Florida plates, is all."

"It was a gift from my son, but what would I want with a fancy car like this?"

"He just gave it to you?"

"A present from a son to his mother. What's wrong with that? You want the car or not?"

"Does your son own the car, or do you?"

"I do. See here on the back of the title where he signed the car over to me."

"Okay. I'll take the car. How about I give you a check for a hundred dollars and you get a New York title to the car. Then I'll come back next Sunday and give you a cashier's check for the balance."

"I don't know. I..."

"I can't take a Florida title signed by your son and made out to you. I'll never be able to get a New Jersey title." I didn't know if that was true or not, but it did seem squirrelly.

The woman looked over my shoulder and started to say something to the guy walking up behind me.

"Look, all I'm asking is for you to get a New York title. You can't sell a Florida car to anyone." Again, I didn't know if that was true or not. I hoped she would buy my story because it sounded right.

"Okay. Okay. I don't want trouble. I'll get a New York title and you show up here next Sunday, same time, with the cashier's check."

Now I had a week to figure out what game was being played. A Florida car, in what appeared to be brand new condition, being sold by a guy's mother in New York for less than half its going price. If alarm bells hadn't gone off in my head then I myself would have been due for a tune-up—of my something's-wrong-here sensor.

First thing Monday morning I called my local police and spoke to the narcotics officer, a Detective Jones.

"So what is it you want from me?" Jones asked, after I explained the deal with the car.

"Two things. First, if I buy it and it turns out to have been involved in drug deals I don't want to be busted. And second..."

"What did you say your name was again?"

I repeated my name, gave him my address and home phone, then added, "And second, I want to be certain that Joey Carguy, the son, is the real owner of the car."

"See what I can do," Jones offered, after I gave him the VIN number. "But I make no promises."

It was only a day later, Tuesday morning, and Detective Jones was on the line. "Here's the deal. The house where the car is registered is located on a canal, easy access out to the Atlantic. House is known for gambling, and the narcs have been watching it for drug smuggling. Guy who owns the car is wanted for questioning, but he took off, left the Audi in the Fort Lauderdale airport long-term lot and flew to St. Thomas and from there he's in the wind. About a week later some guy with the parking stub picks up the car at the airport. Paid cash."

"So, first things first. Was the car involved in anything illegal?"

"Nothing in the narcs' file says so. Can't say for certain beyond that. No one checked it for drugs."

"If the mother registers the car in New York and I get a signed sales agreement from her and register the car in Jersey will I be okay?"

"Better ask a lawyer that question, Mr. Tannenbaum. But I will tell you that if that car has drugs in it, and we find it in your possession, you're in deep do-do."

"From a law enforcement perspective, would you say I'm in trouble if I go ahead with this transaction?"

"If it was me, I'd go find another car. Like I said, if there's drugs anywhere in that car, your ass is toast."

That was good advice, but I didn't take it.

Even if the car had been used to bring a load north, I figured, they'd be long gone by now. And anyway I'd scour the car myself once I got it home.

On Thursday I called the number from the classified ad. "How's title coming along?" I asked, when the husband answered.

"Screw you! To get the title in my wife's name we have to pay tax and a registration fee besides. That's costing us."

"But it's a gift," I said. "Put down zero for the value."

"Can't! Can't prove it's a gift. Tax is close to eight bills, plus the title fee. This deal ain't worth it!"

"Can't sell what you don't own," I replied

"That's a point," he admitted. "So listen here. If I had my way I'd raise the price and sell it to someone not so picky. But the wife says a deal's a deal. Get here by noon on Sunday with your cashier's check, and the car's yours—New York title and all. A minute late and it's gone."

I arrived the following Sunday morning at 10:15. They had the title, and I had the cashier's check in my pocket. In no time at all I was behind the wheel of my new white Audi on my way back to what felt like the sanctuary of New Jersey. But not before I checked the trunk and felt around under the seats for who knows what.

A month later I affixed the New Jersey license plates and the car served our family well, without incident, until its retirement many years later.

Well, not entirely without incident. I did have one momentary scare when the local patrol cop, a man I passed almost daily as he directed traffic in the center of town, motioned for us to pull over.

"Oh, $%#@," I exclaimed, almost loud enough for the cop to hear through the closed window. "He's pulling me over because of the car," I told my wife. "They finally traced the car from Florida. The plates, or something, are on a watch list of some kind. If I get busted for possession of stolen property I'll lose my law license." I was hyperventilating. I should have followed Detective Jones' advice.

"Mr. Tannenbaum?" the cop asked after I rolled down the window.

"Yes."

"I just wanted to thank you for helping Julie get through math and science. She just got her acceptance letter from Rutgers and it's all thanks to you."

At first I had no idea what the officer was talking about. But then it came to me. He was the father of the young girl I had tutored for three years at the local YMCA.

"Math had her beat," the policeman continued, "but you stayed with her. Her grades were high enough to get her into college. Thank you so very much."

"I was pleased to be able to help her," I replied, breathing a sigh of relief.

"Oh, and one more thing..." he added. "Nice car."

In A Car, Under The Bridge

(A Different Kind Of Genius)

Genius comes in all forms.

Buck Scout, a tinkerer extraordinaire, saw gears and pulleys like nobody else. Exercise machines were his specialty, and at one time machines designed by him were the gold standard. These are the machines that allow a user to pull back and hold a bar, or a ring, with little or no force. But when the user moves the bar (or ring) from the "dead" zone, the pull-back force increases almost instantly from zero to maximum. Professionals swear by his designs, and when a new machine comes out, it is mandatory that the other exercise machine companies copy his design so that they can remain competitive.

A man, who I later learned was not Buck, came into my office one morning with a set of drawings. He handed them to me with the statement, "Here is my brother's latest thoughts on an exercise machine to strengthen the lower back."

I studied the complicated-looking sketches for a while, then asked him to explain them to me.

"Not on your life. I've never been able to follow what he does. But it works."

"How do you know it works?"

"First off, all the exercise equipment manufactured by Hercules was designed by my brother. And second, he holds several patents on all that stuff."

"What's his name?" I asked, intending to study all of the brother's patents to see what I was dealing with.

"Buck Scout. My name's James Scout. I own a bowling alley up the road a piece."

"Why didn't Buck bring these drawings himself?"

A funny look crossed the brother's face. "He...he just doesn't do well with people. I handle his affairs for him."

"How do I get ahold of him in case I need to talk to him?"

"Through me," he said, sliding a bowling alley business card across the table. "Just call me."

"Does he live with you? What's the deal?"

"Yes and no. Buck prefers to live in his car. It's parked in the hollow behind the bowling alley. Under the bridge. That's where he works as well."

"He lives in his car?"

"Mostly. Comes up to the alley every now and again for a shower, but we don't see much of him."

I studied the drawings for hours and couldn't figure out how the pulley system worked. I read all of Buck's patents and still couldn't figure out what I was looking at. Pulleys and gears and cords. Looked to me that his supposedly new design was the same as what he had already patented.

I researched Buck and found a newspaper article on Buck reporting that he had been paid several million dollars by Hercules for the rights to the patents.

And he lived in his car!

I called the brother and asked him to have Buck come by the office to explain how the new design worked. I expected a bearded, smelly guy but was pleasantly surprised when a clean-shaven, hair-combed, cleanly dressed young man came through my door. He wasn't much on conversation, but within five minutes I understood what his new design did. And to say it was magnificent in its operation is an understatement. A user could hold any force, say five hundred pounds, with a pinky. And then, by moving the device perhaps an inch, the force would increase from zero to the full five hundred pounds. "Magnificent!" was all I could think to say.

I asked Buck to come back a week later to sign the necessary papers so we could file for the patent. This was going to be a fun one to work on. And it was!

A week later, at exactly nine o'clock, Buck was sitting across from me. I slid the patent drawings to his side of the desk and asked him to look at them. It took him all of ten seconds and he said, "Good."

"So the drawings are all right?"

"Yes."

"Please now read the description of the drawings that I wrote up for the patent to be sure that it's correct as well."

Buck glanced at the ten or so page document, then pushed it back toward me. "It's okay."

"Please read it. It's important to get it right."

"It's okay," he repeated.

I then handed him a pen and began to flip the pages to show him where to sign. But a thought jumped into my head. "Before you sign, would you want me to read the patent to you? You can follow along with the drawings as I read."

Buck looked across to me, hesitated, then said, "I would like that."

And so I read the patent to him and watched as his eyes darted from gear to gear and pulley to pulley as I progressed through the patent. He stopped me twice for corrections. Each one subtle, but critical to the proper functioning of the machine.

When we were finished and the papers were all signed, I asked Buck how he came to invent this particular mechanism.

"I don't know. Hercules came to me and told me the problem. I just see in my mind how the pulleys operate is all."

Sensing his hesitation to leave the office, I asked, "Is there anything you want me to do for you?"

He lowered his head and looked away, clearly struggling.

"Will I get money for this?"

"Of course. The newspaper said you got over a million for your last one."

"I did? I didn't know. My brother takes care of all that stuff for me."

"I sense that there's something more you want me to do."

"Better place to live."

"You're living in a car. Do you want a new car?"

"I want a real place."

"Your own house?"

"An apartment. Can't pay for a house."

My heart broke for this illiterate savant genius millionaire. The least I could do for him would be to secure decent living arrangements. The man had no idea of what his concepts were worth—or even how much money he had made.

"Ask your brother to call me," I said. "He'll fix you up with what you want. Come by this office any time and talk to me if you need anything."

"See you," Buck said as he left the office.

That was the last time I saw the guy and I could only hope that his brother, with a bit of prompting from me, took better care of him going forward than he had in the past.

David Versus Goliath

(Taking On The Pension Industry)

About a month after Mrs. Wiśniewski buried her father, she was informed that the monthly pension checks that had been going to her father would now be going to a woman by the name of Jane Dough. I came to learn that under the terms of the pension, payments would be made for a total of ten years, and if the father died before the ten years was up, the remaining payments would be made to a beneficiary that the father had designated when he was alive—namely this Jane Dough.

Jane Dough, as it turns out, was a former live-in of the deceased father, having lived with him for almost ten years before abruptly disappearing from his life. That was three years back and no one, including the father, mourned her leaving.

The father had not married Jane Dough because the father was still married to Mrs. W's mother. That unfortunate lady had been committed to a mental institution seventeen years earlier, and the law in New Jersey at that time was that one cannot divorce a spouse who is mentally incompetent.

When Ms. Dough went out to run an errand—probably to buy a bottle of whiskey—and never returned, the father went on with his life, likely not thinking much about the absent woman and, as we know, forgetting to change his pension designation.

Once the pension administrators learned of the father's death, they began issuing checks to Jane Dough and mailing them to the address they had on file for her, which was the father's address before he died. But Jane was long gone and the checks were returned as undeliverable.

Mrs. W dug through her purse and produced a very official looking document signed by someone designated as a benefits coordinator. "They wrote me this letter asking if I knew where Jane Dough lived."

"And do you know?"

"Only sort of. Sometime after she left for good some lawyer called my father from some town in Pennsylvania. She was in jail and he was calling on her behalf for bail money."

"In jail?"

"Intoxication. Broke a store window, that sort of thing. From what I gathered, somewhere along the line Jane fell off the wagon."

"And?"

"Dad bailed her out. I think he still had a soft spot for her. Drunk and all."

"Did you give her address to the pension people?"

"I don't actually have any address. My father happened to mention the name of the lawyer and the city where he was and those stuck in my mind, so I do know that. But in any event I didn't answer this letter. As soon as I got it, that's when I called you.

"Listen, Mr. Tannenbaum," she continued, "It's just not right. My mother was married to him all those years while he worked and earned that pension and they're still married. The pension was my mother's just as much as it was his."

"Your mother is in an institution. You said she'll be there all her life. So what..."

"She still needs things. Every month I go up there and bring her things, like slippers, a robe, even pajamas. I give her some spending money so she can buy small things. Why shouldn't she be the one to get that money rather than that drunk? It just isn't fair."

My attempts to get some kind of payout from the pension fund for Mrs. W ran into a brick wall. I made phone calls to the pension administrator, the in-house lawyer for the father's employer, the lawyer for the pension administration company and finally the senior partner of the outside law firm who had been hired to put this matter to bed once and for all. All insisted that Jane Dough was the proper recipient of the pension payments and that the money would be held until they found her.

It goes without saying that I was the wrong attorney to handle this matter. My one course in estates and trusts (even assuming I could now recall what I had learned at the time) was hardly enough background to take on the pension bar. So having failed to achieve anything with my phone calls, I counseled Mrs. W to obtain qualified counsel. I volunteered to help her find someone good, but she insisted I was the right person to fix this for her mother. No amount of begging her to use the right lawyer had any effect on her resolve to have me pursue the case.

The Statute of Wills, I knew, was the starting point for any discussion concerning the disposition of property after a death. For a person to pass a thing of value to another person after his death, the Statute of Wills comes into play, and its provisions must be followed to a T. At a minimum, there must be a written document—typically it's a will—signed by the deceased. The signature must be witnessed, usually by two people, and the witnesses' signatures are typically notarized as well. Lots of formalities—and they are rigidly followed.

None of these formalities were followed when the father

simply filled out a form naming Jane Dough as his new pension beneficiary and mailed the form to the pension administrator.

"Bulls—t!" bellowed the senior outside counsel when I ran my theory past him. "All pension payouts are handled that way!"

"Are you saying it complies with the Statute of Wills?"

"It doesn't have to. It's not a will. It's just a pension designation."

"Was Jane Dough entitled to anything while my client's father was still alive?"

"Of course not."

"Could her father have changed the designation during his lifetime?"

"Of course he could."

"Then nothing passed to Jane Dough while the man was alive. And if that's the case, then it had to pass, if at all, after he died. So clearly the Statue of Wills applies. Period."

"You're crazy, counselor. This is the way it's done. Have a nice day."

Off to the law books. I spent every night for two weeks in a law library reading case after case pertaining to pension benefit designations. The case law was against my client. Case after case cited the proposition that a pension recipient could enter the name of a beneficiary on a printed form and simply mail it in to the administrator without it being witnessed. The cases did not explain why the Statute of Wills did not apply. Instead they all relied on an old New Jersey Supreme Court case from the early 1900s for the proposition that pension plans are exempt from the Statute of Wills. Many of those later cases quoted the language of that old case as saying something to the effect that, "....when it comes to the matter of pensions, the designation of beneficiaries is clearly not covered by the

Statute of Wills."

I resigned myself to the fact that my client was out of luck. But I still didn't know the reason why. I determined to read the original case to learn the rationale behind it, but because it was such an old case, my local law library didn't have it. Undaunted, I drove to Trenton to find and read the original case in the New Jersey Supreme Court's more extensive law library.

Case law book publishers typically include summaries of the legal points enunciated in each case. These summaries are called "headnotes," and they allow people researching a legal point to quickly determine if a particular case is relevant to what they're researching. Sure enough, one of the headnotes that summarized that old case had the language quoted in italics above—the language that the subsequent cases cited for the proposition that the Statute of Wills did not apply to pension beneficiary designations.

Having gone to this much trouble, I settled back and read the case in its entirety. It was long and heavily fact-laden. Near the end, after reading nearly fifty pages, I spotted the portion of the case that had been repeated over and over again as the basis for holdings in subsequent cases. "....when it comes to the matter of pensions the designation of beneficiaries is clearly covered by the Statute of Wills."

Whoa! The actual written decision in this case says just the opposite of what the headnote says. The publisher's headnote writer made a big error. In the actual text of the court's written opinion, the word "not" after the word "clearly" is absent. Thus, the actual holding by the judge in that landmark case was that pension designations are covered by the Statute of Wills.

To be clear, a case's headnotes are not the law. As I said, they are written by the law book publisher as a research aid. The law is whatever the court's actual written decision says. Rather than actually read the case to learn its holding, subsequent judges simply relied on the erroneous headnote. The implication of that error was that every single beneficiary designation in the State of New Jersey was invalid because it was not witnessed as the Statute of Wills demands AND as the fundamental court decision confirms.

"You kidding me?" the senior law firm lawyer said the next morning. "It's well settled law!"

"Go read it for yourself," I replied. "You tell me what it says."

"Tell it to the judge if you think the law is with you! Every pension plan in this state would be messed up! Do you have any idea what this will do if..."

"Let's settle the matter," I suggested, and not for the first time. "Look, Ms. Dough is long gone. Had my client's father thought about it he would have changed the beneficiary. There's a wife who's left out in the cold. Give her the..."

"Can't! Won't! End of story."

"So, what do we do now?" Mrs. Wiśniewski asked meekly, after I explained what I had found and what the pension plan lawyer had responded.

"If you're up to it, we sue the pension plan."

"I can't afford a lawsuit."

"I have confidence you'll win. I'll take my fee out of the proceeds."

"Okay. Let's go for it."

And go for it I did.

The courtroom was packed on the day of the hearing. I didn't know it before the hearing, but every lawyer in the court that day was a pension specialist or a malpractice lawyer. To say there was tension in the courthouse is an understatement. Except the tension was all theirs, not mine. If I won there would be chaos in the pension law world.

JUDGE: Mr. Tannenbaum, I read your brief. Is there anything you wish to add?"

ME: No, Your Honor.

The judge then turned to my opponent, representing the pension plan.

JUDGE: Mr. Senior Counsel, Mr. Tannenbaum is clearly correct. The seminal case says that the Statute of Wills does apply. The headnote, I agree, says the opposite, but that's just the headnote, not the written decision itself. How do you get around all of that?

SENIOR COUNSEL: Your Honor, all the subsequent case law—sixty-five years of case law—says the Statute of Wills does not apply to pension matters. That original case may say otherwise, but the settled law is what we follow.

JUDGE: Why should I follow something that is clearly improper?

SENIOR COUNSEL: Because if you were to rule otherwise then every pension plan beneficiary over the past sixty-five years would be in jeopardy. We'd have chaos going forward. All pension plans, my God, think of all the people who'd have to give money back. Think of the suits. Think of...

JUDGE: That's exactly what I have been thinking about. However, Mr. Tannenbaum has a valid point. These pension plans are contrary to the Statute of Wills and as such appear to me to be invalid. My job is to correct wrongs. And this, on its face, seems wrong.

SENIOR COUNSEL: But the pension plan is not contrary to established case law. It is following the law as we know it to be.

ME: The case law is founded on a clear mistake, Your Honor. To continue to perpetrate a mistake is to further compound a bad situation. I ask you not to do that and to set the record straight going forward.

JUDGE: I'll take this under advisement. You'll have my answer within ninety days. Thank you, gentlemen.

Exactly ninety days later the judge issued his written opinion, which ruled against me. It was a seven-page decision in which he reasoned that the pension right granted to Jane Dough was a present interest in a future payout, subject only to partial divestment month by month by Mrs. W's father. The judge's logic was that because the designation was a completed present gift, i.e. the father had done everything necessary to transfer the remainder of his pension to his girlfriend, the designation stands. Thus, in effect, his pension benefits became Jane Dough's pension benefits, subject only to father's right to collect the pension as long as he lived.

This logic was clearly faulty in my view. Once a gift is a completed gift, it cannot be taken back by the donor. So since Mrs. W's father had the right to name a new beneficiary any time he wanted, there was clearly no completed gift to Jane Dough. Indeed, under the judge's "completed gift" theory, the father had already previously made a completed gift to his first wife and thus could not have re-gifted his pension to Jane Dough.

I'm sure the judge knew all this and that he knew that I was right. But he didn't want to cause a major upset in the pension system. I had the distinct feeling as I read the judge's opinion that he fully expected this to be appealed.

The judge in the Wiśniewski matter constructed a fiction which, if allowed to stand would throw pension law into even further disarray. Think of it; every designated beneficiary of a pension, under the judge's ruling, would own a present interest in the pension. That means a person could not change his/her own beneficiary. Very troubling indeed.

The judge knew what he was doing, because he marked his decision as being "not for publication." Thus, it would not become binding on future cases unless it were appealed to the

Supreme Court of New Jersey, whose decisions are always published and binding. It was a classic punt.

In my mind the judge was actually trying to signal that I was right and that the pension bar better get busy and fix the problem.

But I had lost—at least for now.

"Now what do we do?" Mrs. Wiśniewski asked when I explained the judge's ruling to her.

"We wait a bit," I replied, not wanting to file an appeal to the New Jersey Supreme Court, even assuming I knew how to do so. Which I didn't.

"What are we waiting for?"

"We're waiting for my phone to ring," I replied, trying to sound more assured than I felt. "Their lawyer will call with a settlement offer. They have more to lose than we do. Actually, the only thing that can fix the mess they have is legislation."

"I hope you're right, Mr. T. I'd sure like to get some money to my mother."

It took two weeks, but the phone did ring.

"Here's the best deal we can offer," a junior lawyer at the law firm told me. "Lump sum settlement of fifteen thousand dollars."

The way I calculated the pension they would have paid out about thirty six thousand dollars over the next five years. Even at a discount, this was a low-ball offer. "Twenty-five thousand and you have a deal."

"You kidding?"

"You want to write the reply brief when I file the appeal?"

"That'll be fun."

"You want to explain to the malpractice carriers why your firm got itself in such a mess?"

"Twenty-two thousand is our limit."

"Sold," I said. An even twenty thousand had been my goal. "Of course I have to get my client's approval. But I'll counsel her to accept."

"You mean they'll give us twenty-two thousand right away?" Mrs. W exclaimed ten minutes later.

"Yes, but first I need to locate Jane Dough and strike a deal with her. You okay with splitting this in half?"

"Eleven thousand to my mother?"

"Less my fees. Yes."

"That's way more than I could have expected. Sure, we'll take it."

I called the lawyer in Pennsylvania who had contacted Mrs. W's father for bail money and a week later we had a deal.

Mrs. Wiśniewski was happy.

Jane Dough was happy.

I was happy.

Mother was as happy as a person locked in a mental hospital can be, I suppose.

It doesn't always work out that way.

Guilty, Your Honor...But

(The Wayward Rx Pad)

A friend of mine named Gloria stopped by my house one weekend morning unannounced. "Do you have a few moments to speak with me?" she asked, her averted eyes red from what I interpreted as crying. "Somewhere private."

My wife was at the store and my children were watching TV in the family room. "We can talk in the living room," I said, "no one will bother us there." My guess was Gloria was about to ask me to represent her in a divorce. If so, it wouldn't be a simple divorce by any means because her husband owned a nice business and they had three young children. I resolved not to accept the case, no matter how hard she pressed. She followed me into the living room and slumped onto the sofa.

Having learned not to anticipate, or at least not to display my anticipation, I waited for Gloria to break the silence.

It took her a full minute, but she eventually said, "I know you work with patents and stuff, but you're a lawyer and I need your help."

"Help with what?" I asked.

"I was arrested last night."

"Arrested? For what?" My thoughts turned toward alcohol

and a DWI charge. But I had never seen Gloria drink and I couldn't imagine her being arrested. Maybe shoplifting? Maybe one of the kids slipped something off a grocery store shelf?

"It was all a mistake," she sobbed. "A big mistake's all."

"Start at the beginning," I responded, not knowing what else to say. "What happened?"

A few more sniffles, a wipe of the eyes, head down, she then said, "I was getting a prescription filled over at Corner Drugs, and they asked me to wait a few minutes. And I said 'okay' and walked around the store while I was waiting."

"Here it comes," I told myself. "Shoplifting. The all-too-common I didn't know what I did, it just happened.

"They called my name and I went back to get my prescription. The druggist laid it on the counter and I paid in cash. As soon as I paid, two cops walked over and arrested me."

"For what?"

"They said I was under arrest for obtaining a controlled substance with a forged prescription."

"What was the substance?"

"Oxycodone."

"Oxycodone? Isn't that..."

"My doctor prescribes it for my neck pain."

"You said you had a prescription. Was the prescription for you?"

"Of course! Who else would it be for?"

Now I was really confused. "So your doctor wrote a prescription for you and you were at the pharmacy filling the prescription when you were arrested?"

"Yes."

"Had you filled the prescription previously?"

"Well, of course. But..."

"But what?"

"But not at Corner Drugs. They're open until midnight. I usually go to Park Pharmacy, but they close at seven."

"What time was it?" As if the time mattered.

"Eleven."

"Why so late? I mean Corner Drugs is several miles from your house. Why not wait until morning?"

"I ran out, and...and the pain was getting worse."

"I see," I said, not really seeing anything. In fact, I was totally confused.

"What else can you tell me?"

"Nothing, really."

"Okay, give me your doctor's name and phone number."

I wrote the info down, then asked, "Do you have the name and badge number of the cop that arrested you?"

I wrote that info down as well.

Then Gloria said, "The arrest report will be available later today. I'll bring a copy to you."

"So let me get this straight. The prescription you handed to the druggist was signed by your doctor?"

"I told you it was."

"And it was made out to you?"

"Who else?"

"Yes or no? Was it made out to you? In your name?"

"Of course."

"So why were you arrested? Did they say anything to you as to what you did wrong?"

"Just that it was a forged prescription."

"But you just said your doctor signed it for you."

"That's right."

"Was this your regular doctor? I mean, the doctor you usually go to? Your family doctor?"

"Of course it was. He gives me this same prescription when I run out."

"For how long?"

"Don't really recall. About a year now."

"So why do you think you were arrested?"

"Because they didn't know me at the pharmacy. Maybe they didn't know the doctor either and thought it was a forgery. I don't really know. Oh, this is terrible. Will I go to prison?"

"If you're convicted, this is a felony, which means you could go to prison."

Gloria again began to cry. I got her a box of tissues and waited for her to look up.

"Gloria," I continued. "Please understand. I don't do criminal defense work and I am not familiar with the courts or judges in the county where you were arrested. As your friend, I want you to have a good criminal lawyer. Please let me do that for you."

"I trust you."

"That's exactly why I need to send you to someone good. In fact, I already have someone in mind. I'm the wrong person for this."

"I really want you to defend me. I didn't do anything wrong. Bill (her husband) told me to use you. You handled a business matter for him and he was impressed."

"This isn't a contract matter. Your freedom is at stake here. I need you to listen to me and let me get you someone who knows what she's doing."

"How hard can it be? I handed a prescription to the druggist, who then had me arrested. Bill says we can sue the drug store."

"And you're certain your doctor signed that prescription?"

"Of course I'm certain. Where else would I have gotten it?"

A thought crossed my mind. "You didn't change the amounts of the drugs or anything like that?"

"Of course not!"

"Okay," I agreed, "I'll look into it. But I'm not promising you anything yet."

The police report stated that Gloria was arrested at Corner Drugs at 11:33 p.m. trying to obtain a controlled substance with a forged prescription.

I called the pharmacy and spoke to the druggist. He had a copy of the prescription pad and he admitted it had been signed by a doctor whose name was printed on the Rx sheet.

"So why did you call the police?"

"Because the quantity of pills was too high, and the strength was in excess of what would be prescribed for a woman with Gloria's stature."

"In your opinion, was the prescription forged?"

"I would have no way to know that. Dr. McGee's office is far enough away that we don't get many, if any, of his patients in here. At least, I had never seen his signature before this."

"So you have no reason to believe this was a forgery?"

"Only by the number of pills and the dosage. Not by the actual signature."

"Is that what you told the police?"

"It was."

"Then why do you suppose their report says it was a forged prescription?"

"You'll have to ask them. But no doctor would have signed that prescription for Gloria. That much I'll tell you for certain."

"I don't care what that druggist told you," Gloria said over the phone, "Dr. McGee signed that prescription."

"What about the high dosage and high number of pills?"

"That's what he prescribed!"

Trial day. We were the first case on the docket for the day. Having waived a jury trial, this was all going to be before the judge.

Four people were sitting two rows in front of us in the almost empty courtroom. Two men in suits and two men in blue police uniforms.

"Those two cops," I said to Gloria, "are they the ones who arrested you?"

"Yes."

"And do you know who the other two men are?"

"The one in the blue suit is the druggist."

"And the other?" I asked, a sinking feeling quickly taking hold.

"Dr. McGee."

"That's your doctor, but he didn't say hello to you when he passed by?"

"That's because I stopped going to him after this happened."

"Gloria," I said, turning to face my friend, "if you haven't told me the full truth, now is the time to fess up. Once the trial begins it will be too late. I can get a postponement now if there's something I don't know. Maybe work out a deal. Or at least get you a lawyer who is qualified."

With fire in her eyes, she replied, "I gave you a prescription Dr. McGee signed. You matched it yourself against the one they say is a forgery. You even told me it's the same signature! I was arrested for doing nothing wrong!"

"So why is McGee here?"

"I have no idea. He signed that prescription is all I can tell you."

"Okay, but I never expected the prosecutor to have the doctor in court." In fact, I had counted on his not being here and their not being able to prove the forgery. I had made a big mistake by not interviewing the doctor in person, but when I had requested notes from any conversations or agreements the prosecutor's office had with the doctor, I received nothing. So my assumption was they would not have the doctor at trial.

Wrong! I had been sandbagged big time.

Then an even more devastating thought struck me. Gloria's husband, Bill, was not in the courtroom. Before I could ask her to explain, the trial began.

The druggist was called and testified to exactly what he had said to me on the phone. He also verified the prescription that Gloria had handed him the night she had been arrested. On cross-examination, I asked him if he knew Dr. McGee's signature and he admitted that he did not. He then admitted that he did not know whether or not the signature on the prescription he had placed in evidence was a forgery.

The cops testified to what was in their report and neither could say that they knew the doctor's signature, but that they had acted on statements made by the druggist.

But for the doctor's testimony, the case against Gloria would have been dismissed at this point. Trouble was, the doctor was about to testify.

The prosecutor, a young man seemingly barely old enough to have graduated from college, let alone law school, stood and said, "The state calls Dr. William McGee."

An experienced trial attorney would have objected to Dr. McGee being called to testify, because he wasn't on the witness list and the prosecutor had not given me summaries of their discussions with him. But I remained silent.

After being duly sworn, Dr. McGee testified that at the time in question he had been the doctor to Gloria and her family, which included a husband and three young children. And yes, during the time he was the family doctor he had prescribed Oxycodone to Gloria for pain management. When shown a copy of the prescription Gloria had given the druggist he admitted that it was a prescription written on a prescription pad from his office. His name, address and phone number were printed at the top.

"Did you write that prescription?" the prosecutor asked, his voice a bit tentative.

"I did not," came the firm reply.

The young prosecutor, this perhaps being his first case, then announced, "Prosecution rests."

In hindsight, the prosecutor messed up, and I should have rested as well. I would then have argued to the judge that the charge of forgery had not been proven beyond a reasonable doubt. It's not clear how the judge would have actually ruled because, one the one hand, the doctor had testified that he had not written the prescription in question, but, on the other hand, no one had testified that it was not his signature.

But that's in hindsight. Wearing my best Perry Mason face, I approached Dr. McGee and asked him to look at the prescription form that had been entered into evidence. He did so. I then instructed him to tell the court if that was his signature.

In a clear voice, Dr. McGee said, "Yes, that is my signature on the prescription form."

With perhaps a bit of triumph in my voice, I then said, "Defense rests."

After all, this was a forgery case and the doctor just admitted that he had signed the prescription form. Thus, there could not have been a forgery. Gloria was going back to her family a free woman. Perry Mason had nothing on me.

The baby prosecutor then stood. "Re-direct, Your Honor?"

"You may, counselor, but only to the question of signature."

"Yes, Your Honor. Now Dr. McGee, you just said you signed the prescription pad. When you did so, was there a prescription for Oxycodone on the paper?"

"No there was not."

"Please explain."

"Well, I had fallen into a bad habit of signing my name to blank pads and leaving the pads in my different examining rooms. That way, my nurses could write out prescriptions without waiting for me to finish with patients."

Why Dr. William McGee wasn't arrested on the spot is beyond the scope of this writing. McGee then went on to explain that several of his pre-signed pads had gone missing, and at least one such pad was discovered missing shortly after one of Gloria's visits.

"Dr. McGee," the prosecutor then asked, "would you have ever prescribed Oxycodone for Gloria in the dosage shown on the prescription in front of you?"

"Objection," I weakly called out. "This is beyond the signature question."

"Overruled," the judge said. "Answer the question."

"Never."

"And what about the quantity?"

"Objection," I tried again.

"Overruled."

"Far too many. That amount could very well prove lethal."

"Prosecution rests."

The hole was already far too deep. "Defense rests," I stammered, the Perry Mason strut totally gone.

I turned to face Gloria. Her head was down, tears were streaming down her face.

"May I approach the bench, Your Honor?" I asked.

"You may."

When the prosecutor and I were both in front of the bench, I said, "It may appear that my client is guilty, Your Honor, but..."

Before I could say anything further, the Judge leaned forward, looked directly at the young prosecutor, and said in a sharp tone, "I suppose you promised the doctor not to report him to the medical board in exchange for his testimony?"

The young man standing to my right timidly nodded his head in acknowledgement.

"Did you turn over a record of your conversation with the doctor to Mr. Tannenbaum as I note he requested?"

The prosecutor consulted his file, flipped a bunch of pages, and then, his face turning red, confessed, "I can't find where we did."

"And Mr. Tannenbaum, I suppose your client lied to you about that prescription." Not waiting for my reply, he continued, "I am prepared to grant her a new trial, based on the prosecution's failure to produce what Mr. Tannenbaum requested, but it seems clear to me that while she may not have forged the doctor's signature, neither did he prescribe that amount of Oxycodone. You have an addict on your hands, and the sooner she deals with it the better. I can't imagine the outcome of a new trial being any different. And next time, the prosecution will get it right. But frankly, sentencing her to jail with a family and all doesn't seem right. How about instead of a new trial I order her into a rehab program and upon graduation all proceedings in this matter will be sealed. Mr. Prosecutor, are you on board with that?"

"I am, Your Honor," the young guy said, obviously happy not to have to inform his bosses as to how poorly he had performed.

The judge looked in my direction.

Without hesitation, I said, "I can't imagine a better outcome, Your Honor."

Throw Him In Jail Your Honor

(Just Kidding)

When I first began defending pro bono drunken driving (DWI) cases, I won every single one of them. It didn't matter how drunk the client was, how much damage he caused, or how much of a toot the guy was, I got him off.

I started to compare myself to Perry Mason, who also never lost a case, and it was all I could do to keep from thumping my chest when I walked out of the courtroom with another notch in my belt.

But then, about two years into my perfect record, the New Jersey Supreme Court took direct aim at the judges who heard DWI cases. It seems that judges had been taking pity on defendants who spent money on lawyers and thought anyone who hired a lawyer had been punished enough. The Supreme Court told the trial judges to stop that practice. And stop it they did. From that day forward I never won another DWI case. For that matter, I never again won any traffic-related court matter. I went from an unblemished win record to an unblemished loss record by one edict of the upper court.

So much for Perry Mason. I was now in league with the Washington Generals and even they won a game once in a blue moon.

So the stage was set for when my wife was given a traffic ticket for passing a stopped school bus. But the ticket was wrongly issued. The school bus was discharging students on a highway several yards beyond an intersection, and my wife was driving on the intersection road. She stopped at the highway, the school bus being stopped on the edge of the road off to her right, and then proceeded to cross the highway and turn left. She never passed the side of the bus. From the perspective of the cop who issued the ticket, however, it appeared that she had driven past the bus, albeit on the opposite side of the road, when in actual fact, she had come from across the highway out of the side street.

"Pay it," I said when she asked me to defend her. "I haven't won a traffic case in five years, and I see no reason why that is about to change."

"We're moving out of New Jersey and I don't want a traffic ticket on my record. I didn't pass that bus. And besides, it was off the road and didn't have any flashing lights on."

The question of flashing lights on or off was, in my mind, a he said, she said issue and the judge would side with the cop. "I still say pay it. It's not worth fighting it"

"It is to me! The hearing date is set for the night before we leave. It works out just fine. Just go up there and tell the judge."

"But..."

"I know your record. This is your chance to leave with a winning record. You can't lose them all."

One case doesn't a winning record make. But the discussion was over. I had lost the argument.

New Jersey is the state with the highest population density and consists of innumerable small towns abutted against one another, each with its own government, police and fire departments, and judicial system. The town in which the ticket had been received was tucked away in the hills just off

Route 22, and I had routinely driven through its picturesque downtown on many occasions. I had never appeared in its small courtroom, which doubled as the town council chambers when the court was not in session.

The night we arrived, the chamber was filled to the proverbial rafters, with people spilling out into the lobby. The ticket business in this burg was booming.

"May as well wait out here," a kindly-looking gentleman suggested. "They're doing arraignments now and traffic won't start for another twenty minutes or so."

I just had to ask. "How do you know I'm not here for an arraignment?"

"Not in handcuffs, now are you?"

"Might be a lawyer."

"You look lost. Lawyers are lots of things. Lost isn't one of them."

"You seem to know your way around the court house."

"Gotten more than my fair share of tickets these past few months I have."

"Alcohol will do that."

"How'd you..."

"You're right. Lawyers are lots of things. Been defending more than my fair share of DWI's."

"Hey, you're a lawyer. How about taking my case. Judge is about to throw the book at me."

"My advice. Duck."

"Take my case."

"You don't want me."

"Why?"

"Long story. But you're right. I'm lost."

My wife and I entered the courtroom before he could respond. There were no empty seats, so we stood along the back wall and listened while the judge, a white-haired man in his early sixties wearing the expression of a person who has seen this movie a thousand times, listened to an explanation as to why a man, his hands shackled together in front of him, should be allowed to roam the world a free man without posting bail. His story was that he and his friend had robbed a drug store but had an agreement that guns were not to be used. Unfortunately, a gun fell—or was dropped—while the two of them ran toward the door.

When the man stopped talking, the judge, without looking up, said, "Bail request denied. Remanded to county jail. Next matter. And let's speed this up; we have a full house of summonses to work through."

"Okay, Your Honor. How about if we pause with arraignments and work through the tickets? The perps can hold a bit longer."

"Good idea. Clerk, call the first summons matter."

According to the notice taped to the wall next to me, our case was the twentieth on the list. After listening to the first two I leaned toward my wife, "Let's work our way up toward the front. This is going fast. He's finding everyone guilty. Hope you brought your checkbook."

"Summons number GP1002-4590 Tannenbaum," the Clerk called out a few minutes later.

"Is the police officer present?" the judge asked when we approached the bench.

"No, Your Honor," the clerk responded.

"I assume you are here to contest your case and not plead guilty."

"That's correct, Your Honor," I answered.

"Okay, then, we'll have to postpone this until we can schedule the officer. See the clerk and work out a time. Next matter."

"Lock him up, Your Honor!" The voice came from the town prosecutor sitting at the counsel table behind me.

"I should lock him up?" the judge asked, clearly as befuddled as I was.

"May I be heard?" the prosecutor said, now standing at the counsel table.

"You may," the judge said. "Bailiff."

Two uniformed men began walking in my direction.

The lawyer, not moving from counsel table, said, "I have it on good authority that Mr. Tannenbaum is preparing to skip out of the state later this week." After a long pause he continued, "This horrific ticket will remain unpaid and the citizens of this good town will not get justice. I ask the Court to hold Mr. Tannenbaum in the county jail until we can resolve the matter fully."

I was dumbfounded. First off, I was the lawyer, not the defendant. If anyone was to be held it was my wife, not me. But more important, neither of us should be held for any reason, not at this stage. It was true we were leaving, but...I was confused, to say the least. How did he know?

"New Jersey is about to lose a very fine lawyer and two good people. We can't allow that to happen, Your Honor. You can stop this injustice simply by putting Mr. Tannenbaum in jail until he comes to his senses and agrees to remain in the state permanently."

I finally turned to face the prosecutor and to my surprise I saw that he was a man I knew fairly well. What I hadn't known was that he was this town's prosecutor.

I turned back to face the judge. "Your Honor," I began, "I..."

"Say no more, Mr. Tannenbaum. Is it true you are leaving the state?"

All my training screamed for me to say nothing. Demand a lawyer. Shut up. But instead, I simply said, "Yes."

"Then I am afraid the prosecutor is correct. I cannot allow you to leave while this matter is pending, now can I?"

"I see..."

"So you agree. Well, the prosecutor has suggested jail time. I'm inclined to agree."

"But..."

"But there is another way this can be handled," the judge said, a slight smile forming.

Yeah, throw my wife in jail?

"Want to hear how that will work?"

Can't wait. This is going from bad to worse. "Certainly, Your Honor."

"I will call the case one more time. If the police officer does not appear then I'll have no option but to dismiss the matter. Is that okay with you and your client?"

"It is not okay with the prosecutor," my friend said, his hand now on my shoulder. "I want this man to remain in New Jersey."

"Please proceed," I said to the judge. "It is okay with us."

The Court called the matter again and of course the officer was not in court. The judge, true to his word, dismissed the case.

So in the end my wife was right. I was leaving New Jersey having won my last case, if a dismissal for failure of the complaining party to appear can be called a win. But not before my heart had taken a solid jolt.

FUN IN THE SUN

(Or Perhaps Not)

After changing planes in Jamaica at Montego Bay, my wife and I arrived at our destination, the capital city of Kingston. The town Harry Belafonte was so sad to leave. The overhead airport signs read JAMAICIAN CITIZENS TO THE LEFT, NON-CITIZENS TO THE RIGHT. The only two people from our plane going to the right were my wife and I. Well, actually, I was the only person going to the right because my wife had detoured off to obtain Jamaican currency, which, as it turned out, was U.S. dollars. Piece of cake, I told myself. We'll be through immigration and on to our hotel in no time.

I handed my immigration card to the uniformed customs inspector who, having no other business, took his grand old time. Every single person in the citizen line had moved past their inspectors while mine was still studying my papers. After what seemed an eternity, he looked up, studied my face as if committing it to memory like a detective at a crime scene, and said, "You checked 'pleasure' as your reason for coming to Jamaica. Is that correct?"

I certainly hadn't come for work, and for five of the seven days it was certainly correct. But I did have an appointment with the finance minister. Was that pleasure? I certainly hoped it would be. "It's accurate. I'm here on a vacation."

Silence.

I think I would still be standing there if another inspector hadn't approached. He had one more bar on his shoulder than my guy. "Problem here?"

"When was the last time anyone from the States came to Kingston for pleasure? Montego Bay, no problem. But not here."

"Not very often," the senior guy agreed. "Not for a long time."

"This guy claims he's here for pleasure."

Now two uniformed officials were glaring at me.

"Go through his bags," the second guy instructed. "If you find anything suspicious, arrest him."

I hesitated to think what items a customs inspector would find suspicious. But I knew I was about to find out. What I didn't understand until later was why it was suspicious for a person to come to Kingston for pleasure.

The first guy accompanied me to the luggage pickup point. "This your suitcase, mon?" he asked. He had a fifty percent chance of getting it right since there were only two suitcases, one with my name on it and one with my wife's.

I nodded.

"Put it on the counter and open it."

I did as instructed.

"Why is this in here?" he said, pointing to what were obviously women's things. "These are not yours and they look new."

"They're my wife's," I said. "Some of her stuff is..."

"Clearly you are here to sell these. I should have you arrested."

My sense was that the only reason I hadn't already been arrested because this guy was angling for something to line his pockets. "I'm not here to sell anything. They belong to my wife."

"You are alone. No wife."

I pointed across to where my wife was discussing something with the currency exchange clerk. "That's her over there."

When my wife was brought over, the inspector held up a pair of undies and asked if she recognized them.

"That's mine, yes."

"Why is it in his suitcase?"

"Didn't all fit in mine."

"Open your bag, lady."

I bent to lift my wife's bag and the inspector grabbed my arm. "It's her bag, you say. Let her open it."

The good news was that the second bag was indeed crammed full. But that didn't stop him from throwing almost everything out onto the counter. A tantrum in slow motion. The man apparently had made up his mind that we were here to sell goods and he was obviously counting on a big attaboy for having caught us.

"Find anything?" the boss asked a few minutes later as he also began pawing through my wife's clothes.

"Nothing much."

"Okay, then," the boss said. "Pack it up and get out of here. Enjoy your pleasure in town."

What the inspectors knew, but I didn't, was there was very little, if any, pleasure to be had in Kingston town. Maybe that's why Belafonte had sailed away planning not to be back for many a day.

Our initial destination was the Pegasus Hotel, an elegant structure not far from the government offices. Elegant, yes, but surrounded by a barbed wire fence with armed guards stationed at the massive entrance gates that swung open and closed with each entering or leaving vehicle. Once in the building, we were warmly greeted and welcomed to Jamaica. We were told that the hotel had made a reservation for dinner in their "world famous" club at the top of the building.

"I thought we'd go out and see the town," I said to the manager. "Have dinner in a local place."

"I don't advise it. We have the finest dinner..."

"Please arrange for a cab in one hour," I said, tired of being pushed around.

Not the smartest idea I've ever had. A cab was indeed waiting at the appointed time. The driver, having been already briefed, knew exactly what we wanted and did his best to accommodate. He stopped at a lovely little restaurant and had us sit in the cab, the doors locked, while he went inside.

"They are ready for you," he announced when he returned. All is in order. You can go in now."

"I'll be right here if you need anything," he said as we stepped from the cab. "When you're done with dinner just come out. I'll be here."

"No need. We'll call a..."

"Orders! I'll be here."

"In that case," my wife said, "come in and have dinner with us."

And he did. A most delightful dinner it was, I might add. Among other things, we learned what a Jamaican (at least this Jamaican) likes for breakfast, a dish called ackee fruit and saltfish, usually with boiled dumplings. And for dinner it was curried goat.

After dinner we asked our driver to show us the town. At first he refused, citing hotel orders. But after I opened the door as if to exit from the cab he relented and took us to a shopping plaza. I had visions of folks dancing the limbo, their wild colored shirts flowing in the breeze. Instead, bearded men, their hair braided to their knees, yelled, "Beat it, mon. You're not welcome here!"

Still not convinced, we got out of the cab and took several steps toward some music, only to come face to face with a group of wild looking young men, their eyes clearly focused on my wife, and one of them wielding a machete. I signaled to our driver and after the exchange of a few choice words between him and the men, we were back in the cab speeding toward the hotel.

The next morning, we learned that a man had been shot by the guards after he had climbed the hotel's fence. I didn't know whether he was coming toward the hotel or going away, but at that point I didn't much care.

"You'll have to bear with us for a bit, I'm afraid," explained a waiter. "A new government has been elected, and economic times are bad. The ministers are struggling to maintain order, but people have nothing."

The finance minister kept me waiting in his outer office for over an hour. Others came and went while I sat. It's a common tactic when one party wishes to soften up another, in order to show who's boss. The minister had no worries on that part. I was as soft as they get, and I knew who was boss. If I hadn't known before our plane landed, my experience with customs and the barbed wire around the hotel pointedly reminded me that Uncle Sam was far to the north. I kept listening for the whistle from Belafonte's boat and wishing I were on it, leaving Kingston town in my wake.

A booming voice bellowing, "Bring him to me!" interrupted my reverie, and a moment later I was ushered into a gigantic office. Standing behind a huge desk was perhaps the tallest and broadest human being I had ever seen. Seven feet two inches was my guess and maybe 350 pounds. Perhaps even taller and heavier.

He might have been a giant, but he was anything but jolly.

"So!" the finance minister boomed. "You are the person responsible for our drop in tourism. Tell me why I shouldn't put you in jail to rot."

A lawyer should not throw his client under the bus, but my client was safely back in the States, and if there was ever a good time to do it, this would be it. So throw I did.

"Mr. Minister," I began, glancing around for furniture to jump behind should one of his hammer fists start in my direction. Or would he use a machete, like the one that guy in the mall last night shook over my head? "Please don't confuse me with my client and his wife. I had nothing to do with those airport flyers and I did not advise them to do that."

"You are the lawyer. You are responsible."

"Responsible to obtain money for injury to my client. Not for disrupting tourism. I wasn't even their lawyer when all that was going on."

"Do I have your promise there will be no more disruptions?"

At this point I'd promise this guy anything. "Absolutely."

"We'll see. Sit!"

I sat.

"You extorted a lot of money from us and you place me in an awkward position."

"That was an insurance settlement," I countered.

"Our government has strict controls on money leaving our country. I cannot allow such large sums to flow out for no reason whatsoever."

"It was my understanding the money was paid by an insurance company, based in Lond..."

"In this country it is all one in the same. I cannot allow money to flow out from here."

"But...but," I stammered, "that money was in settlement of a terrible injury that..."

"I'm not interested in your sob stories. I have a government operation to run. Your client is a rich American doctor. I have starving people, and you are draining our resources!"

This guy is going to blow at any minute. Wish I had registered my whereabouts with the American embassy. This is not looking good.

"Give me a plan for that money in the bank account, and do it quick. I'm thinking to take it all back. I should never have allowed that in the first place."

I did, in fact, have a plan for the money, based on the last conversation I had with Janet before boarding the plane.

"Doc's been thinking about your trip and the Jamaican bank account," Janet had said. "I know I told you to go buy a condo, take vacations down there, but he says he wants that country out of his life forever. He says knowing you have a place down there, or are vacationing down there, will drive him crazy."

"So?" I responded. "Want me to cancel the trip? Give the money back? What?"

"If Doc had his way, yes. But here's what I want. Use the money to pay for your hotel and stuff and buy jewelry. Any jewelry you pick will be fine. Spend it all in this one trip. No going back"

"You mean you want me to bring back a hundred thousand dollars' worth of jewelry?"

"Exactly."

"Won't that be a constant reminder to Doc?"

"You just bring back the jewelry," Janet had instructed. "I'll deal with Doc."

Now looking directly at the finance minister, I asked, "How about if I bought jewelry with the money?"

His eyes bore into mine. "A hundred thousand dollars' worth of jewelry?"

"Yes, minus my hotel bills."

"All from island merchants?"

"All from island merchants."

"If I release the money to you, how will I know what you will or won't do with it?"

"You have my word," I replied. "Just jewelry and my hotel bills."

"Here's what I will agree to," the minister said after a long pause. "You use your own money to buy the jewelry and before you leave the island you present me with all the invoices and I will release the money to you."

I'll be out a hundred grand, which I don't have, and I will never see this guy again. Not a good plan. "I don't have that much money."

"You're a rich American lawyer. You have the money."

Arguing over my net worth was not going to advance the quickly deteriorating situation. "I have an idea," I said, trying to stall being thrown out of the giant's office. "How about writing a note authorizing me to use the money from the Jamaican bank account only..."

"Better yet." He reached for a business card, wrote a number on the back, and thrust it at me. "Go buy what you want. Have the storeowner call me at this number to approve the purchase. I will give him the bank account number, so it will not be necessary for you to front any money. I will approve jewelry only, so don't try anything or I'll..."

"Don't worry. Jewelry only and my hotel bill at the Pegasus and at the Half Moon Resort in Montego Bay."

"Okay. No nonsense."

"No nonsense," I agreed, trying to keep my hand from being completely crushed by his parting handshake.

So now the worst was behind us, or so I thought. A few pearl or diamond necklaces, a couple of Rolex watches, some brooches and bracelets, all diamond studded, of course. Throw in a few cufflink sets and voila! One hundred thousand dollars spent and then on to the beach.

It proved not to be so easy as all that. We started with the gift stores in the Pegasus and branched out to the supposedly upscale jewelry stores recommended by the hotel manager. But remember that no tourists come to Kingston. The only pearls in their jewelry stores were plastic. And when we asked about diamonds, the response was "Mon. This be Kingston. Nobody don't wear any diamonds here."

So, after a full day of buying everything in Kingston that seemed to have any real value, and having each proprietor call the finance minister and get the okay from him—an okay that perhaps included a 'finder's fee' for the minister—we had spent a grand total of nine thousand dollars.

On to Montego Bay.

The Half Moon Resort knew we were arriving to buy jewelry and volunteered to keep our purchases in their safe, along with the jewelry we had bought in Kingston. In fact, we were met at check-in by both the hotel manager and the owner of the hotel stores, who was armed with a complete list of everything we had already purchased. "Please join us in the store when you are ready," he said. "We have better merchandise here than over at Kingston."

"What about watches?" I asked, trying for high value items. "Perhaps Rolex."

"I will have them here for you in the morning," was the cheerful reply.

I had visions of Rolex watches displayed for sale in New York's Chinatown, the most expensive one selling for twenty-five dollars. On closer examination, the name behind the slightly cloudy lens read: R.olex. I couldn't wait to see the brand name on this guy's watches.

Just as the shop owner claimed, his merchandise was of a higher quality than we had seen in Kingston. In fact, several of his bracelets and necklaces were stunning. A magnificent Rolex showed up two days later and we bought that, too. We also bought several other watches, all with high gold content.

New merchandise showed up each morning for three days in a row, and we bought everything of value. We still hadn't spent more than forty thousand dollars. But local merchants began showing up in the lobby, some with goods in burlap sacks and some with notes to come visit their stores in town, and we bought from them as well.

The day before our flight home, we took a cab into town and bought a necklace from one vendor and several rings from another. Even with our hotel tab yet to be calculated, I figured we still had more than thirty thousand in the bank account that would be lost if we didn't do something.

We started to walk out of the last shop and the proprietor motioned for us to join him in the corner of the store. "I know you have money in an account," he began, his eyes darting back and forth in classic clandestine fashion, "and I know you can only spend it for jewelry."

"How..."

"Never mind how I know. This is a small island. People are related. I have a shop in Miami Beach, and we move money back and forth all the time. Write me a check on the local bank, and I'll deliver the money to you in the states."

"I don't have checks."

"Just write it on a piece of paper. Put the account number down and the amount. And sign it. You'll have your money in the States in one month's time."

"And what will your charge be for this...service?"

"A thousand dollars."

And I have a nice bridge to sell you too. The problem was from my perspective that I was leaving Jamaica in the morning with instructions from my client that this was a one-time excursion and any money not used would be left behind. I didn't know if Janet and Doc would change their minds, but in the meantime, those were my instructions, so I had nothing much to lose.

"Give me a pen and paper," I said. "You have a deal."

I handed the man my business card along with a handmade check and told him I expected the money to be in my possession within a month.

"It will be there. I give you my word as a businessman."

It wasn't clear to me that the bank would honor my handmade check since they seemed to be privy to everything, including the finance minister's instructions, but that was the jeweler's problem. My problem, of course, was that thirty thousand dollars rode on the word of a Jamaican businessman. Besides which I had just violated my agreement with the finance minister.

Sometime about three in the morning, I sat bolt upright in bed, recalling the words, On this island we are all related. Finance minister's brother-in-law, for sure! I had to hope that my new business partner was nothing more or less than who he said he was. Otherwise, we would no doubt find ourselves at the wrong end of a machine gun when we reached the airport and attempted to clear customs.

"Did you buy anything while on the island?" the uniformed guard asked as we were passing through a checkpoint to our gate.

"Some," I answered.

"Show me," he demanded.

"Here is a list," I said. Everything had been neatly wrapped by the clerks and I hoped not to have to undo it all. But no such luck.

"Open what you have!"

This is a ploy by the finance minister, I told myself. He allowed us to buy this stuff, knowing full well we'd be stopped on the way out of the country, and everything will be confiscated. And I'm helpless to stop it. Keeping out of jail is your real concern here, so cooperate.

Open the packages I did. "I want to see receipts for every item," he demanded, as the pile of unwrapped jewelry on his counter got bigger and bigger. "No one buys this much stuff. You are not leaving this country until we get to the bottom of this."

"Here," I said, digging out the finance minister's card. "Call him."

"He's our boss! If this were legal he would have issued us an order. Wait here."

And there we were, with our jewelry sitting bare naked on the counter and we, some distance away, standing against a wall with three policemen on guard, one armed with an automatic rifle. If anyone had grabbed a watch on his way past, we would have been helpless to prevent it.

Finally, a new uniformed inspector arrived, this one with a white cap and at least four shoulder bars. "You two," he called. "Gather what belongs to you and come with me."

We both began stuffing things into our hand luggage, not taking the time to rewrap them. "You have it all?" the man asked, when we straightened up.

"I think so," I answered, glancing around to make sure that a box of earrings or cufflinks had not gotten left behind.

"Then follow me," he instructed. And off he trotted at a brisk pace.

"Have a good flight," he smiled, as he escorted us to the front of the line at our gate. "The airline has upgraded you to seats 3A and 3B—first class. Come with me and I'll get you settled."

The episode at the airport had so unsettled me that even after the plane was high over the deep blue Caribbean, I had visions of the Jamaican Air Force forcing us back to Kingston town. This time neither "business" nor "pleasure" would be the proper box to check. "Prison" would be more like it.

Never in my life have I been so happy to touch down on U. S. soil. I didn't exactly kiss the ground when I came down the ladder to the tarmac, but I might have had not a man from the U.S. Customs Service been standing there waiting for us.

It was all good. Before we left Jamaica, I had called the Customs Service to tell them we were coming. I had three things in mind. One, I didn't want to open all that jewelry right there in the terminal for everyone to see and hoped to be afforded a private space for it to be inspected. The thought of not making it to my car at JFK had crossed my mind. Two, I didn't have enough money or credit cards to pay the import taxes on a hundred grand of jewelry. The solution I could think of was to have my son drive out to the airport with my checkbook. He'd have to be allowed to meet me at customs, which, even then, one could only get to by flying into the country, not by driving into the airport from the road. And three, I wanted the U. S. Government to know we were in Jamaica and raise questions if we didn't appear on time.

"I'm Deputy Director Hicks of the U.S. Customs Service," the man announced. I'm here to escort you personally off the plane. Just tell the cashier the value of the goods you're importing, and he'll calculate the duties."

"You don't need to see anything?"

"Anyone who calls ahead and alerts us can't possibly be in the business of smuggling. So, unless you're prepared to prove me wrong, just declare the value, and you'll be on your way. And by the way, your son is waiting at the cashier."

And with that, he was gone.

* * *

Three months went by and no check from the Jamaican businessman. I called the island several times, but no luck. It turns out, though, that he actually did have a store in Miami Beach. I called, and the phone was answered by someone with the same surname, claiming to be my guy's brother, but professing to know nothing about my $30,000. I told him to check with his, ahem, "brother" and to call me back.

A month later, no call back and needless to say, no $30,000.

I called again, and the same man said that his brother had no memory of any such transaction or any handmade check.

"I bet his memory improves after a call from the finance minister," I said.

Of course, I'd have been a fool to clue in the Jamaican finance minister as to what I had done in violation of the agreed spend-it-all-on-jewelry-plan. Who knows what he would have done? I would never have chanced it, no matter how far away he was.

But the bluff worked. All thirty thousand dollars ultimately appeared in my bank account.

And one other note: Doc loved the jewelry. He was never seen without the Rolex on his wrist.

So much for his hatred of everything connected to the Island In The Sun.

Talent Rules

(Creativity At Its Best)

"I got a new client today," I said to my wife over dinner one night. "I'll be going out to California to meet him later in the week."

"Oh, who is that? The last time you said you had a new client it was Bugs Bunny."

That was when I represented Barney and Chuck-E-Cheese, or as Mary called them, the large fuzzy animal crowd. This time it was a real live person. "Guy by the name of Dan Aykroyd."

Mary's eyes lit up. "Dan Aykroyd!"

"Yeah, you know who he is?"

"I can't believe you don't!"

"Why should I know him? What's he done?"

"You're not kidding, are you?"

"No. Who is this guy?"

"You know. Saturday Night Live? Ghostbusters?"

Truth is, I didn't watch much TV—unless a ball was involved—and I had no idea what a ghostbuster was.

"Do you even know what he looks like?"

"No, how would I?"

"He's famous. And famous people are not introduced. So

when he comes in the room you need to know who he is, or things won't go well."

"You have a suggestion?"

"We go to Blockbusters and get as many Dan Aykroyd movies as we can, and you watch them until you recognize him."

Good plan. We got a pile of movies and I binge-watched for three nights, starting from the oldest. By the time the plane took off we had watched all but two or three.

Mary's prediction came true. I was waiting in his agent's office when Dan swept in without introduction. Truth is, his appearance had seemed to change with each movie we watched, so I was nervous that I wouldn't recognize him despite my marathon study session. But there was no mistaking the charisma surrounding the man. He gave off an aura in a way I had never experienced before, and when the door opened and he strode in, the room suddenly filled with an energy that wasn't there before.

"You must be the trademark lawyer," he said, his hand extended in greeting. "This promises to be an exciting project. Let's adjourn over to the house of my friend Joe Lyons where we can be private. The other side will be there and Mrs. Lyons [a celebrity in her own right] has agreed to set out a working lunch."

"Suits me fine," I said. "We can negotiate the terms anywhere."

"Great. And just to give you a time frame, this must be signed today by seven o'clock, because my wife and I are going to the opening of her new movie tonight. She'll drop by to say hello later in the afternoon."

The movie Dan was referring to was Wayne's World. His wife, Donna Dixon, did indeed drop by with their infant daughter, stayed for about an hour, then excused herself to go home in preparation for the opening.

The negotiations were difficult, and for many hours I was holed up with opposing counsel, hammering out details of who can do what to whom, and who gives what to whom, and when the money is paid, and when accounting takes place, and on and on.

Lunch was served in the dining room around two, and at Dan's suggestion we continued negotiations while we ate. At one point I got up to stretch my back and stood behind my chair. "Please don't mind me," I said. "If I sit too long, my back gets stiff and that's not good. I'll just stand for a few minutes and that'll loosen it up. Let's just go on with the discussion of payment terms."

"Hold for a moment," Dan said from across the table. "Do you have a swimming pool at your home?"

I said I did. Then Dan said, "When you get home, hang sand bags over your shoulders and around your neck. Get in the pool and hang in the water. The sand bags will stretch your spine. Works wonders. Do it three times a day for two weeks."

The advice had come in a serious tone and without a trace of a smile. Yet I knew he was pulling my leg. "Sand bags around my neck sounds like something I'd not want to do."

"I can understand that," Dan replied without hesitation. "So instead you must fasten weights to your waist and stand in the water five times a day for three weeks. Be sure to do the first set before breakfast for best results."

"Now that I can manage," I said, trying my best to be a good straight man.

The negotiations continued until six, when Dan stood up. "Okay, we're finished," he announced. "Counselor, get this all drawn up, and I'll sign on Monday. And get the trademarks and whatever else you need filed around the world as soon as possible." With that, he was gone.

Having been dismissed, I caught a ride to the airport and flew home to Dallas. True to his word, he signed the contract, although it wasn't on Monday, it was on Thursday.

"We have one more Aykroyd movie to watch," Mary announced the next night. "You up for it?"

After having spent time with Dan, I thought it would be fun to then see another movie of his. The movie was The Couch Trip, where Dan plays a guy committed to a mental institution who breaks out and substitutes for a psychiatrist on a radio show. In the movie, the radio show with Aykroyd playing the doctor becomes wildly successful.

Halfway through the movie it hit me. When Dan had been giving me back pain advice across the lunch table, he had slipped into the nutty Couch Trip radio doctor and I hadn't picked up on it. He had known right then that I wasn't as much of a fan of his as I had wanted him to believe.

Oh, well.

About a year later, my wife and I met up with my high school best friends, Don and Fran, for the pre-opening event of an entertainment venue in which Aykroyd had an interest. Suddenly, and without warning, Dan Aykroyd stepped out from behind the curtains where a band was playing. He spoke to the large crowd, told a few jokes, and promised he would appear the next night for a performance. I turned to my friends, saying, "Hey guys, you want to meet Dan Aykroyd?"

"Yeah, sure," Don said. "Right!"

Reluctantly, Don and Fran, with my wife trailing behind, followed me as I tried to catch up to Aykroyd's detail. I finally managed to move through the crowd and came upon Dan just as he was leaving the venue through a back door. "Hi,

David," he called. "Are our trademarks protected around the world yet?"

With that, he turned and joined his entourage as they beat it from the building.

"Now do you believe I represent him?" I asked my friends.

"I suppose so," came the response, their attention already on the next band to take the stage.

About six months later, I called Mary at her office. "Hey, honey," I began, "drop what you're doing and drive down to Reunion Arena. Find the train tracks and I'll meet you there. It'll be worth your time. Promise."

What I didn't tell Mary was that Dan Aykroyd was going to be there. Dan's friend, Lyons, the man whose house we had negotiated the contract at, had located an abandoned train car that had belonged to a distant relative, a railroad magnate. The old railcar had been moved to Dallas from the cornfield where it had been left to decay and was completely rebuilt: bedrooms, sitting room, kitchen, baths, everything. Today was to be its maiden trip from Dallas through Austin, San Antonio, and then to New Orleans. And Dan Aykroyd was to ride along on the Dallas-San Antonio leg.

I arrived at the train siding about an hour before Mary said she could be there and was given a tour of the newly refurbished interior. Dan arrived during my tour; we exchanged a few words, and he went out to the rear platform of the railcar to relax while I went off in search of Mary.

Fifteen minutes later, I escorted Mary into the train car, beginning at the front end where the kitchen was located. We worked our way back past each sleeping room and a common room and then out onto the back platform, where two guys were deep in conversation. Mary nodded to them and began to step down the three-step ladder leading to the ground.

"Mary, hold up a moment," I called. "Want you to meet someone."

Mary dutifully turned around to face me. "Mary, this is Dan Aykroyd. Dan this is my wife, Mary."

Aykroyd removed his sunglasses and held out his hand. I don't recall what he said, but I do recall that Mary very nearly fell off the platform.

About that time, a diesel engine approached from the front end and gently bumped up against the train car. Mary and I quickly climbed down from the platform, crossed the tracks, ducked under the fence, and watched from the parking area where a small crowd had gathered.

A few moments later, the train car slowly began moving forward, but not before Dan Aykroyd, never one to miss an opportunity to entertain, stood up and before our eyes transformed his six-foot-one frame into a five-foot-five Ross Perot caricature.

Perot was at that time running for U. S. president, and Aykroyd then proceeded to deliver a political speech that would have made Perot proud.

How a man with the physical stature of Aykroyd can make an audience believe they are looking at a man half his size is beyond me. The transformation had occurred right in front of our eyes, just as Aykroyd's transformation into the nutty psychiatrist had occurred across the table from me, all very seamlessly.

Talent rules!

DOES NECESSITY BEGET INVENTION?

(Not Always)

I've worked with inventors for over thirty-five years, and early on I came to appreciate, and admire, the creativity constantly on display. From the start, I would have told you that the old adage "Necessity is the mother of invention" was always true. In some instances, the invention is, in fact, a creative solution to an otherwise troublesome problem. But in other situations, the invention comes before the problem is even known. Two examples come to mind, one belonging in the "necessity" camp, and one, well, one illustrating an elegant solution before its time.

Example One: In the late sixties, a fire occurred in a lower Manhattan high-rise office building, destroying two floors of the building. Businesses had to close for months while the floors were being rebuilt. Forensics traced the fire's cause to an overheated wire buried at the center of a very thick bundle of wires in a telephone utility closet. To prevent future fires of this type, it was necessary to remove unused wires from such wire bundles. These unused wires were the result of people moving and telephone numbers changing, and there was an ongoing problem with the cable bundles getting larger and more tangled as time went on.

Problem: The sheer number of tangled wires within a bundle, and the fact the bundle snaked around many turns, made it impossible to remove unneeded wires from that bundle.

The only apparent way forward was to disconnect all the live wires and essentially rewire the entire office building. That would entail turning off thousands of phones for an extended period of time. Not an acceptable alternative.

Solution: Find a loose end of a wire to be removed. Slip a metal cone, or "bullet," over the loose wire end so that the bullet (which has a hole in both ends) slides along the wire. Connected to the trailing end of the bullet is a flexible tube. Pushing on the flexible tube causes the bullet to slide along the wire to be removed. Eventually, the bullet is not able to move forward because the cable jumble is too great.

Smoke, make it red smoke, is then blown into the open back end of the flexible tube. The smoke travels inside the tube to the bullet and billows out of the cable bundle at the point where the bullet is stuck.

A worker then digs into the cable bundle at the point of the smoke, frees up a forward path for the bullet, and continues to push the tube, with the bullet still attached until it is again unable to move. This procedure is repeated until the bullet emerges somewhere down the cable jumble. Then the dead wire, which has thus been encased within the tube, is pulled out through the tube. In this manner, the old wires inside a tangled cable bundle can be removed without turning off phone service.

I was fascinated to have been able to work with the clever inventor who came up with this idea and to secure a patent for him. He solved a real problem in an elegant way and prevented major inconvenience to a whole host of people and businesses. A tip of my hat to him.

Example Two: This was a breakthrough discovery that solved a real problem, only the inventor, at the time of the invention, wasn't trying to solve anything. He was just being curious.

On Wednesday, August 1, 1979, a young man stuck his head in my office. "Got a few minutes?" he politely asked. "Have something to show you."

He was carrying an empty glass Coke bottle. "You can throw that here," I offered, pushing my trash basket in his direction.

"Oh, no. This bottle is why I'm here." He then proceeded to hold the bottle up to the light with the open top end pointing toward my face. "Look at the rim around the opening. What do you see?"

Perhaps a shadow flitted around the rim. Perhaps nothing. "I'm not sure I saw..."

"Look again."

This time it was clear. The rim had lighted up as if light was trapped inside the edge of the rim. "There's light in the rim," I said, puzzled as to why this intrigued a research scientist.

"It's actually trapped in there," he said. "I was in the park on the Fourth of July having a picnic with my family. I picked up a Coke bottle and noticed that when I clamped my hand around the bottle like I'm now doing light would emerge from the top. When I opened my hand, the light went away. Like this."

The light was now gone.

He was obviously excited about what he had observed, but I had no appreciation for his enthusiasm. But what I did know was that Bell Laboratories only employed the best and the brightest, and the best and the brightest didn't get excited over seeing light at the end of a bottle unless it meant something more than just a parlor game.

"So, what's that mean?" I asked. "I need a little help here."

"Total internal reflection," he answered, as if that explained it all. "The phenomenon is called total internal reflection, and it happens when light that would normally pass through the glass is trapped because my hand is there, and stays within the glass. The trapped light travels to the edge."

"So, what..."

"It took me a while, but think of a TV screen. Light comes out of the screen. What if I put a piece of glass, or better yet, a flexible membrane, in front of the screen? Light from the screen flows into and through the membrane. The membrane would have light sensors around its perimeter." He paused, giving me a chance to extrapolate to the next step. But seeing that I wasn't yet on board, he continued. "Then if I touch the membrane at a certain spot, the membrane is depressed and the light from the screen is trapped inside the membrane by TIR at the point where I touched the membrane. The trapped light then flows to the edges of the membrane and impacts the light sensors."

The bell finally went off in my head. "And by monitoring the sensors, you can calculate exactly where on the screen you touched!"

"Bingo! And then you could have the TV, or computer, put questions (or answers) on the screen in various locations, and when a person touches a question (or an answer) the sensors would determine which question (or answer) was touched."

The inventor was ultimately awarded U.S. Patent 4,484,179 on November 20, 1984.

As a P.S. to this story, before I could file for the patent, another inventor popped into my office. "I understand you're the attorney preparing a patent on a touch screen."

"I am," I agreed.

"I saw the clunky glass they're using up there and thought of a better way. Simply imbed the edge detectors on the screen and you won't need a separate plate of glass."

"That's difficult to do," I replied, wondering where this was going.

"Come up to the lab. I've been working on putting light sensors around a CRT screen. See for yourself."

Ten minutes later we were in his lab, and sure enough, there was a clunky old TV up on a metal table with something I took to be aluminum framing all around, wires hanging out from all sides.

"Give me a few minutes to power this contraption up, and you'll see for yourself what I'm talking about."

Sure enough, a few minutes later the TV screen came alive with a series of questions, each having multiple possible answers. The inventor touched the C answer and the image on the screen changed to say, "You just touched the C answer." He repeated this a few times and then asked me to do the same. Each time that I selected an answer, the TV confirmed what I had selected.

Keep in mind this was more than twenty-five years before the iPhone was introduced, and frankly, it felt a bit odd to be poking a piece of glass and having a machine accurately know what I was telling it to do. Sure, I had been controlling computers with a keyboard for years, but this was up close and personal—and while others may have already been experimenting with touch screens, to me this felt very, very different.

U.S. Patent 4,346,376 covering the improvement over the initial concept was granted on August 24, 1982.

The use of total internal reflection as a way of detecting the presence of a finger on a screen did not ultimately win out as the best commercial approach and was superseded by other technologies. But I tell you this story anyway, because it demonstrates the kind of creativity and out-of-the-box thinking that I was so privileged to have been exposed to throughout my career as a patent attorney. My inventor was certainly not the first to observe light coming out the end of a Coke bottle when he wrapped his hands around it. But he was the first to realize what no one before him had realized, namely, that the concept of total internal reflection could be harnessed for a particular productive purpose.

One other quick anecdote on the subject of inventor creativity. I had no part in this little adventure other than to inform our paralegal late on a Friday afternoon that a certain patent application had to be signed and filed no later than Monday. That meant getting the inventor's signature on the formal papers over the weekend.

Unbeknownst to me, the inventor lived two and a half hours north of where the paralegal lived and was leaving early Monday on a business trip. "Not to worry," the inventor said to my paralegal when she called to arrange for the documents to be signed the next day, Saturday. He suggested that they meet at a Garden State Parkway plaza that was more or less halfway between his house and hers.

Once on her way the next morning, however, the paralegal realized that she didn't know what the inventor looked like, how old he was, or anything else about him. This was long before the advent of cellphones, so calling him en route wasn't any kind of option. The more she thought about it, the worse her sinking feeling became. Garden State Parkway plazas are notoriously busy on Saturday mornings, as the Parkway is a major route to the beaches of the Jersey shore.

She arrived at the plaza fifteen minutes early, sat in her car until one minute to ten, and then proceeded up the steps toward the restaurant in what she believed would be a futile effort to rendezvous with the inventor.

Not so!

There, standing just inside the door, was a man in a white shirt, his right hand high in the air, clutching a pen.

Play Money

(Weekends Are For Lawyers)

"Hi, call me Jenny," the white-haired woman announced when my assistant ushered her into my office for the first time.

Jenny had been referred to me by a partner who represented a trust company. The trust company managed a trust in which Jenny was a beneficiary. I never did learn the true relationship of all the players, but piecing together things Jenny told me, I deduced that her father had been blessed with an oil fortune. Whether he was a wildcatter, a developer, or a landowner was never clear to me.

Jenny was, in her own words, "a mathematical savant." Indeed, she could multiply or divide any complex set of numbers instantaneously in her head. I could not keep up with her even by using a calculator. I simply couldn't enter the numbers fast enough.

Jenny told me that she had developed a method of teaching others how to perform such mathematical feats and had been in negotiations with the federal government to introduce the method in schools across the country. My task would be to complete the negotiations with the feds and then to negotiate licenses with all fifty states for use of Jenny's system.

Anxious to learn how to multiply 24638912 by 84593021 in my head, I asked Jenny to show me how it's done. I couldn't imagine why in the world I would ever need or want to accomplish such a feat, but the thought of being able to do it fascinated me.

"Not so fast, Mr. T. I didn't bring the materials, so that will have to wait for another day. Today I just wanted to meet you to see if we can work together. After all, we'll be traveling around the country, and possibly around the world, and that means we'll be together a lot of hours. I need to know if we're...compatible. Are you married?"

"I am."

"What will your wife think about us being together so much?"

"You'll have to meet her, and you can ask her yourself."

"Is that possible?"

"Of course."

"Maybe next visit. Let's talk now."

And so we chatted about her and about math and how she envisioned the arrangement with the feds would be.

"Okay," I replied, after our conversation slowed. "When you decide if I'm okay, just let me know. I'll be here."

"Oh, I've decided already."

"And..."

"And you'll do just fine."

"So, can you tell me the method? Just outline it for me."

"On my next visit, I'll show you what I have." Jenny abruptly stood and marched out of my office. No "goodbye," no "see you soon." No nothing.

"What was that about?" my assistant inquired after Jennie flashed past her without so much as a nod of the head.

I explained what had taken place and asked her to ask my partner what he knew about her.

"Already did that. He referred me to the investment banker who just said he pays Jenny's bills and to send him our invoices directly."

On Monday I called the banker myself, confirmed that he was paying the bills for Jenny, and asked what he could tell me about her.

"One thing I can definitely tell you is that she likes you and looks forward to working on her project with you. You know, of course, she's a gifted mathematician."

"That much was clear. But what I'm curious about is her intent to teach her talent in the schools. It just doesn't seem possible."

"Jenny is unique. I have every faith in her."

"What she outlined will be expensive, especially if we have to negotiate with every school district in the country."

"Money's no object, if that's what you're worried about. Just itemize your invoices."

"Do I need to clear expenses with you up front?"

"Not necessary. If they get out of hand, I'll let you know. Oh, and Jenny flies first class, so arrange your own plans accordingly."

"Is there a number where I can reach her? She didn't leave any information with us."

"Through me will work. Jenny spends most of her time in Colorado. I'll call you when she's available. All appointments will be made through my office. Anything else?"

I didn't know what else to ask. "That's it for now."

Four weeks later, Jenny was back in my office. The meeting was on a Friday afternoon, as the first meeting had been. The banker's office had called at eight-thirty in the morning, saying Jenny would be in town for the weekend and asking if I could meet with her at four. I was available. So here we were.

But Jenny didn't have the materials with her. Instead, she wanted to talk about her plans for teaching her concept and how it would be rolled out across the country. She walked out of my office at six sharp.

Another month passed, and this time my assistant got a call late Thursday afternoon, setting up a meeting for four the next day. I had anticipated the call and had asked my wife to be available for dinner. When I told Jenny about dinner plans, she was cool to the idea at first, but when it was time to leave to meet Mary, she became enthusiastic.

"You know," Jenny said to Mary at one point over dinner, "I will be spending time with your husband. Is that okay with you?"

"Why shouldn't it be?" was Mary's answer, which seemed to stump Jenny.

At the next meeting a month later, Jenny brought the first chapter of her materials, and after a brief discussion of the table of contents, the conversation turned again to the rollout. Try as I might, I couldn't wrap my mind around exactly what it was we would be rolling out. "Exactly what agency will we be negotiating with?" I asked.

"Department of Education, of course," she said.

"When do you expect that to occur?"

"When you're ready. You are far from ready. You don't even know how I plan to teach my method, so how could you possibly negotiate a proper deal?"

Jenny had a valid point. But the problem with her point was she wasn't allowing me to learn her method. "Good point," I acknowledged. "So how about let's go over the method now so I can..."

"Time's up. It's six o'clock. Don't we have dinner plans?"

"We do. And my wife will be joining us again."

"Oh, how lovely. I hope you have a nice place selected."

"You like fish?"

"If it is prepared correctly, I do."

"Well, I've never known this place to do anything other than prepare fish correctly," I answered, having no idea what prepared correctly meant to Jenny.

Mary, who holds a master's degree in electrical engineering, thoroughly enjoyed meeting Jenny the first time and listening to her talk about mathematical concepts, and was looking forward to dinner and discussing math with Jenny again. I guess the fish had been prepared to Jenny's liking, because she said nice things about the dinner. In fact, that was all she would talk about, and no matter how hard Mary tried, it was clear that any math discussion was off the table.

"You know," I said to Mary after dropping Jenny off at her hotel, "the only time she comes to my office is at four o'clock Friday afternoons. And it seems like its once a month on the fourth Friday."

"Like a weekend pass?"

"Exactly like a weekend pass. A monthly weekend pass at that."

Jenny's next visit went pretty much the same as the previous ones, except as we were dropping her off after dinner she handed me a stack of material to read. Finally, I'd get a peek into her secret sauce.

Not so. What I found were detailed, school-district-by-school-district rollout plans, all very neatly overlaid on a national map, but nothing about the method itself.

This meeting-and-dinner routine continued like clockwork on the fourth Friday of each month for seven more months. The only change was that the meetings had expanded to three hours. At the end of what was now over a year, I didn't know much more than I had the end of our first meeting. And I told Jenny so.

"Patience, Mr. T. Rome wasn't built in a day. This is a colossal undertaking. Imagine if every student could multiply and divide the way I can. Imagine how the world will change."

Actually, calculators and computers have all but eliminated the need for doing complex math, whether in one's head or otherwise. But Jenny wasn't having any of that. I called the trust banker and explained the situation, telling him it was a waste of money to continue paying me for three hours of my time month after month. We were going nowhere.

"You're getting paid, aren't you? I haven't asked you to discount your hourly fee. In fact, feel free to raise your rate if you like. If you want, we can reimburse your firm for dinner as well."

"It's not that," I replied, "and I certainly appreciate your prompt payment." He actually had been paying the invoices within two days of receipt. "But I'm not performing any legal service for her and I feel...well, I feel bad about that."

"On the contrary, Mr. Tannenbaum. Mountain Estates reports a major improvement in Jenny's...Jenny's disposition. You are doing wonderful work."

"What did you just say?"

"Short answer. Keep it up. Jenny needs this."

Where have I heard the name Mountain Estates? Is it a ski lodge in the Rockies?

"It's a psychiatric facility for psychotic rich people," my assistant informed me a few hours later. "From what little I could find, it seems like this is where rich misfits are accommodated."

I called Jenny's banker to break the news that I had no intent of continuing as Jenny's therapist, or whatever role he saw me playing. But before I could say a word he told me that Jenny wouldn't be coming to see me anymore.

"I spoke to her doctors after our last conversation," he said, "and they agree it is better for her to break off the relationship than for you to do it. I again thank you—and your wife—for the great year you both gave Jenny. She hasn't been this happy in a long while."

NOBEL LAUREATES
ARE AWESOME

(And Well-Traveled)

Nobel laureates in physics are awesome, beyond being scientific geniuses.

I came to understand this when a Nobel Physics prizewinner was engaged by my law firm to be a technical expert in litigation. I won't even try to describe his area of expertise — first because it wasn't my case, and second, frankly, because I can't, then or now, even pronounce the words describing his expertise.

Because of a scheduling conflict, no one from the litigation team was available on a particular night to accompany Professor Laureate to dinner. That's a big no-no in law firm circles, and as the dinner hour was fast approaching, a litigation partner stuck his head in my door.

"Hey, David. How would you like to take Professor Laureate to dinner tonight?"

"Who's Professor Laureate?"

"The technical expert in the Silva case."

I knew the Silva case was big and important, but that's all I knew about it. "What's his expertise?"

"Nobel laureate in blah blah blah."

"What's that?"

"Never mind. Can you take him or not? We're up against it, and for me to split one of the team off now would be... well, not good."

"Who else will be there?"

"On your own. He's delightful. You'll enjoy."

"You owe me one." With that, my partner quickly retreated down the hall.

"Hey, Honey," I said when Mary answered the phone. "You available for dinner with a Nobel laureate tonight?"

"Tonight?"

"Just found out. You joining me?"

"More notice would be nice."

"Just got the assignment. Should be fun."

"What do I do with Kat?"

Kat is our granddaughter whom Mary and I were raising. She was a high school freshman at the time. "Ask her to join us if she wants. Would be a good experience for her."

A moment later, Mary was back and announced that Kat would indeed be having dinner with us. "Tell her his name, but don't tell her what he has accomplished. You might suggest she look him up." My hope was that Kat's curiosity would send her to the computer to look Laureate up.

"Knowing Kat, she'll sit and draw during dinner anyway. When was the last time she joined in the conversation?"

Kat was (and is) an artist. She's done several of my book covers, including this one. "Join in the conversation?" I replied. "Not often, that's true, but with Kat you never really know. Professor Laureate's staying at the hotel across the street. I walked to work today, so pick us both up at the hotel at seven. I'm thinking of the Warwick Room at the Melrose. It should be quiet there."

I was standing in the hotel lobby at seven when the professor arrived. We shook hands, and before I could say anything further, Mary and Kat pulled up into the driveway. Frankly, I was surprised to see that Kat had actually come, even though she had said she would. Going to dinner with firm clients was not her idea of a way to spend a perfectly good evening. But there she was. And wearing a smile to boot. Well, to be fair, Kat was never a pouty teenager; she was just quiet and reserved.

Mary had climbed into the back seat with Kat by the time we got out to the car. Quick over-the-shoulder introductions, and we were off across town to the Melrose, where we were immediately ushered to the requested corner table. It was a light night at the Melrose, and we had a vast chunk of restaurant real estate to ourselves.

Before the menus came, Kat commented on some species of animal I had never heard of. Under questioning later, Kat explained that she had learned about the animal, and that it was going extinct, from watching Animal Planet. But at the time, Mary and I sat in silence as Kat solicited the professor's views on what should be done to help this and all animals similarly situated.

To my surprise, Professor Laureate listened intently to Kat's ideas, and then when she fell quiet, he offered his own thoughts. Within a few minutes, the exchange between them expanded to include the socio-economic situation of the indigenous people of the island where this particular species had lived. The only break in their conversation came when the waiter stood over them politely waiting for a food order which neither of them seemed terribly interested in providing.

Their conversation had moved on from animals to sociology, to the political structure of the island. Then on to the flora and fauna of the South Pacific, with Kat commenting on species of plants and animals I thought she had made up until the professor confirmed that she was right about most of what she had said. He then filled in numerous minute details that even Kat didn't know.

The dinner came, was consumed, and the plates removed, and still neither Mary nor I had uttered a word other than to the waiter. Finally, I turned to Kat and asked how she know all this about the South Pacific. Animal Kingdom—and follow-up on Google—was her reply.

Not wishing to appear to be picking on my granddaughter, I directed the same question to Professor Laureate.

"Oh, American Nobel winners travel as unofficial ambassadors. I've been on every continent and have spent considerable time on the islands that fascinate your granddaughter. I hope someday she can travel there herself."

I thought that the conversation would end there, but not so. Kat began anew, this time with comments on the wildlife and peoples of New Zealand. Within minutes the two of them were again going at it hot and heavy, exchanging thoughts and ideas. This interaction didn't let up until we were parked in front of the professor's hotel and the doorman had opened the car.

"Had a delightful time tonight," the professor said in parting. "Your granddaughter is delightful. I wish her well in school."

"Do you know who that was?" I asked Kat as we drove away.

"Of course I do. I looked him up on the Internet. He won a Nobel Prize in physics for blah blah blah."

I didn't understand a word Kat had just said, just as I hadn't understood any of what my partner had said earlier. "So why were you talking about the birds and bees of the South Pacific when his expertise is clearly in physics?"

"I didn't want him talking about stuff none of us know anything about. I didn't know he studied the flora and fauna of those islands."

"And the civics as well."

"At least I could keep up with him on that stuff."

As I think back on it, that was one of the most enjoyable dinner conversations I have ever been part of. And I barely said ten words.

There's a lesson in there for me somewhere.

Not All Ties Are Created Equally

(Some Are More Equal Than Others)

"What's in a tie?" you ask.

Well, even if you didn't ask, I'll be happy to try to explain. I didn't know it at the time, but hindsight has such good vision I now can't believe I didn't see this coming sooner than I did. But I didn't.

Or more to the point, I didn't want to see my client for what it was—a knock-off merchant. In late spring, they would prowl the alleys of Hong Kong or Singapore, looking for unscrupulous manufacturers who would sell overruns for the upcoming holiday season.

It worked this way: A US merchant, like a toy company, would design an item such as a Sesame Street doll (after securing the appropriate license) and then would contract with a Hong Kong factory to make, say 500,000 dolls. Except the factory would not stop at 500,000, but would crank out maybe 600,000 of them. Along comes my client, Knockoff, Incorporated, which buys perhaps 10,000 dolls at a fraction of the cost paid by the toy company, which has spent design money and promotional money, and if the doll is hot—think Tickle Me Elmo—Knockoff, Incorporated, makes a killing.

If Knockoff sells enough of the dolls to be noticed, they receive a cease-and-desist letter somewhere around February. And, in the normal course of events, they do, in fact, cease and desist, while meantime having made their money over Christmas. Except, come late spring they again dispatch their buyer to Hong Kong to buy some other "overruns" for the next Christmas.

In fact, in many situations it's actually a close call as to whether Knockoff did anything wrong. Often, the problem is with the factory in Hong Kong making it seem as if the things they're selling are their own design. In many situations, those things are generic-looking, and selling them in the U. S. is perfectly okay. That doesn't stop cease-and-desist letters from being sent, or lawsuits from being brought. My involvement with the client, at least initially, was over several of these "almost generic" items that were defendable. So I ended up across the table from many an irate lawyer trying to calm things down. I settled some, bluffed many, and generally speaking, my client prospered.

Then the crap, as they say, hit the fan.

It seems that the wife of a famous artist, let's call him Rembrandt, was shopping in a high-end department store and came upon a good-looking tie, the pattern of which had been lifted, so she claimed, from a book of artwork authored by her husband. Off she trotted to the family lawyer, who then caused my phone to ring.

"What the $%#& does your client think he's doing, ripping off a man such as Rembrandt? They have their nerve!"

Not the best start to a day, but not the worst, either. At least the process server wasn't waiting in the lobby. "This is the first I've heard of this, so let's take it from the top," I responded, stalling to get my bearings.

The problem was, he was at the top. There wasn't much more to it. I learned about the wife's visit to the department store, and the lawyer sent a fax showing a picture of the tie along with a copy of the artwork. Seems Rembrandt is known for his bird sketches, and he had published books of such drawings. World famous, I was told.

The next morning, FedEx dropped off a tie that I dutifully matched against several bird sketches from a book of Rembrandt's drawings I got from the library. I couldn't find a conclusive match. My client insisted he bought the ties from a catalog of an Italian tie maker. I was ready to do battle.

"Send over a copy of that catalog," I said to Knockoff, "I want to put this one to bed before they file suit."

A few days passed, and no catalog. When I confronted Knockoff, they said they could no longer find their copy, and the manufacturer had none either. The sun was getting to this old fish.

I sent a paralegal across town to the library to check out Rembrandt's other three bird books. I held the tie up against every picture in all three books and found no match. I called the other lawyer and told him what I had done. "Cut the tie open so it lays flat and check again. It ain't hard to find the match."

Twenty pages into the first book, there it was. A perfect match, right down to the shading on the bird's wings and the tones on the beak. The kicker was that it wasn't just a single bird; it was a male and female pair of blue jays, both matched perfectly to the tie. I had no doubt that it had been copied. No doubt in the least. And more importantly in my mind, neither would the jury.

Apparently, the department store lawyers had come to

the same conclusion, because they had removed all the ties from their several stores and were preparing to handle any lawsuit brought against the store by bringing my client in to defend them. They put me on notice as to that.

"You may not know this," I told my client, "but if the court finds this to be willful, and I have every reason to believe it will, then the judge can impose a hundred thousand dollar penalty for each instance."

"So..."

"So, how many ties did you sell the department store? I know it's more, but for sake of discussion let's just say ten. That would be a million dollars."

"They can't..."

"They can...and they will."

"What do you suggest?"

"Settle."

"How much?"

"Twenty-five thousand."

"What?"

"Look, this goes much further, and my firm'll be asking for double that as a retainer alone. The other side won't sue you; they'll sue your customer. The customer will bring you in, and you'll end up paying their legal bill as well as ours. On top of that, you'll end up paying a half million or more to Rembrandt. You're looking down a million-dollar barrel. Now that I think of it, I think you'd better make that settlement offer fifty thousand."

"You nuts?"

"Look, won't take a jury but two minutes to decide those birds were copied straight out of that book. And when they do, you'll..."

"So, that's the manufacturer's problem. And they're in Italy."

"Did they give you an indemnity when they sold you the ties? Which is to say, will they defend the lawsuit?"

The resulting silence told me all I needed to know.

"I'm thinking Knockoff is on the hook here all by its little lonesome. Am I right?"

"Okay. Okay."

"Okay, what?"

"Settle it. Maximum fifty."

An hour later I had Rembrandt's lawyer on the line. "My client's willing to settle. Twenty thousand."

"Listen to me. Money's not the issue here. Rembrandt's never commercialized his art. He abhors folks who do. He's a purist. Ties with his art on them in stores is beyond the pale. Guy's blown a fuse."

"Ties are out of the stores now," I reported. "Only a few have been sold."

"No deal. We're preparing a suit. Knockoff is a rip-off company. This will teach it a lesson."

"Your guy's an artist. Artists hate lawsuits. He gets on the stand, no telling what'll come out. Maybe he didn't draw those birds himself. Who knows what we'll find on discovery?"

"No deal."

"Twenty-five thousand. Delivered to his house in the morning."

"He's on vacation up in Cape Cod. Spends the summers up there."

"File suit and the depositions will mess up his summer. Tell him the FedEx truck will be there by ten tomorrow with twenty-five thousand. That should get him out of his funk."

"I said no deal."

"Just tell him. I need an answer by four, five your time, if he wants that check in the morning."

"By law I have to tell him, but I doubt he'll accept. I'll let you know."

While I waited I had a release agreement drawn up and ready to go. The lure of fast cash is a universal enticement.

An hour later I had my answer.

At five I called the client. "Here's the deal. Cut a check for twenty-five thousand made payable to Rembrandt." I gave him the address on Cape Cod. "A signed release was faxed back to me a few minutes ago. But it's contingent on that check arriving by ten a.m. So, drive it to the FedEx office if need be, but don't miss the cutoff."

At nine thirty the next morning, I was handed a fax that read: "Check arrived. The contingent release is now final."

Later in the day, the client called to say he wouldn't be using me going forward. I had cost him too much money.

EAT, DRINK AND...

(So Much for YOU, Major Murphy)

One facet of building and maintaining a law practice is to interact with clients and potential clients outside of business hours. To that end, my wife and I often hosted eight- to ten-person dinner parties in our home. The purpose, of course, was to get to know each other in a social setting, thereby fostering mutual respect and trust. These gatherings usually went off without a hitch.

But not always.

Murphy's Law—named after the U.S. Air Force R&D officer, Major Edward A. Murphy, Jr.—tells us that "anything that can go wrong will go wrong." And there were any number of occasions at these gatherings that the ghost of Major Murphy seemed very much a part of the festivities. But fate—or sometimes my resourceful wife Mary—often stepped in to save the day, Murphy's Law notwithstanding.

Like the time, Alex, a valued patent client, broached the subject of expanding his company by acquiring several of his competitors. He would need to hire a law firm with merger and acquisition experience, and several of my partners fit that bill perfectly. After careful thought, I decided that William Jenkins was the partner who best matched Alex's personality and his needs.

I thought that the best way to introduce Alex to William was to invite them, and their spouses, to our home for dinner. To round out the dinner party we also invited Ginna and Franklin Wolkerson. Franklin had just founded an online grocery store, and Ginna was CTO of an infrared card reader company. Alex used IR detectors in one of his products, so we had common ground.

Alex showed up a few minutes early and apologized for coming without his wife, who had taken ill at the last moment. Alex and I sat in the living room sipping champagne and nibbling bruschetta. Alex animatedly told me his plans for Target A, his first acquisition, even though he was still months away from approaching the target.

Ginna and Franklin arrived about ten minutes later. Just as I had thought, Alex and Ginna hit it off instantly. Their conversation quickly turned to the exciting prospects IR promised in the world of electronic detection. For my part, I learned from Franklin about the complexities of accepting grocery orders over the Internet and delivering the selected items on time.

Soon after, my wife ushered my law partner William Jenkins and his wife, Gloria, into the living room, but with Murphy's ghost sneaking in behind.

At the instant my partner entered the room Alex's face went white, followed by a facial expression that screamed, "Was this done on purpose?" As my wife was about to introduce William to Alex, Alex stood, a smile now on his face, his hand thrust out in greeting. "Nice to see you again, professor. It's been a while."

Now it was my partner's turn to have a strange look on his face.

"It seems you two have met," I said. "I didn't know that. And this is Bill's wife, Gloria," I managed to add. A confused look also flitted across Gloria's face, but it was gone in an instant.

"I've not had the pleasure of meeting you before, Gloria, but I certainly know your husband," Alex said, addressing Bill's wife.

"How are you doing, Alex?" Bill asked, his smile beginning to fade.

I still was not certain if he recognized Alex, but judging from the strained expression on Alex's face it was best to leave that subject alone.

The conversation resumed all around, what with talk of electronics, groceries, and the Dallas Cowboys' latest adventure. The dinner itself went off without a hitch. Dessert was served, and around eleven the guests all left, except for Alex. Other than that strange encounter at the beginning, all had gone as well as could be expected.

"So you know Bill Jenkins," I said to Alex, as I poured him one last drink. I was curious as to the dynamic that had played out between the two men. "I suppose from a prior life?"

Alex drained the Scotch, wiped his lips with a small napkin, then said, "I certainly do, David. He's the professor who flunked me out of law school many moons ago."

So much for trying to increase our firm's work from Alex's company. Kiss that acquisition work goodbye. Now I would be lucky to even hold on to the work I had. Not the way I had hoped the evening would go. In the world of "you win some, you lose some," it was clear which heading this dinner party fell under.

"I don't talk about that phase of my life," Alex continued. "But yes, I went to law school. Professor Jenkins was my contracts law professor. And yes, he flunked me out. This is the first I've seen him since."

So much for the careful selection of Bill to match Alex. "I'm terribly sorry," I offered.

"Don't be. You had no way to know," Alex said, pausing in our entranceway. Was he deciding to fire me on the spot or wait until Monday? The look on his face was indeterminate. Monday seemed to be winning out.

"You had no way to know this," he continued, "but it was a dream of mine to be a lawyer. A dream since high school, maybe even before. Professor Jenkins told me I was not cut out to be a lawyer. He gave me failing marks to prove it."

"Still..."

"No, David. Truth is he was right. I'm a businessman. And if I say so myself, a very good one at that."

"You are indeed. This is actually your third business, right?"

"Fifth. But who's counting?" He paused, took a step toward his car then turned back to face me. "You know, Jenkins did me a big favor. Steered me in the right direction. I'm glad he did it. I love business. Have a good one."

I watched as his Maserati slid gracefully out of my driveway.

So much for you, Major Murphy, I thought to myself. Things don't always go so wrong.

On another occasion, one of the invited guests was an inventor of very low carbohydrate desserts. What I hadn't known, and what came out during the dinner conversation, was that Mrs. Inventor had developed her products because she herself could not digest carbohydrates.

My wife's menu for the dinner party was shrimp and roasted vegetables primavera over pasta.

Needless to say, Mrs. Inventor picked around her dinner plate, quietly eating the veggies and shrimp and very little else. That's when the story behind her invention came out. And that's when my wife pulled me aside whispering, "I made bread pudding for dessert. What a disaster!"

It took a moment until the vision of a well-fed Major Murphy laughing at me dissipated. "We have a supply of her frozen desserts in the freezer. Serve them along with yours," I suggested.

"What a nice surprise," Mrs. Inventor exclaimed when the desserts were served. "And enough for everyone to enjoy. How very thoughtful of you."

Beat you again, Edward Murphy.

Then there was the time we hired someone to come in and help in the kitchen because the menu required precise timing. Murphy must have been the one to answer the phone at the catering service that Mary called, because the service sent a bartender instead of a food handler. Nice man, but an icemaker was his appliance of choice. Stoves and ovens were far outside his wheelhouse.

The invited guests, including two CEOs and their spouses, arrived pretty much at the appointed time, and between hors d'oeuvres and the unflawed performance of the bartender, everyone was in a good mood as we moved to the dining room for dinner. Soup was served, and the conversation continued unabated. Soon the soup dishes were replaced by salad plates all around.

The conversation was spirited, and all seemed to be going well, when my wife, who had been in the kitchen, poked her head into the dining room and motioned for me to join her.

"We have a problem," Mary stage-whispered when I joined her in the kitchen, nodding in the direction of the bartender, now the acting sous chef. "I asked him to put the Cornish hens in the oven when I served the soup, which he did, but I had turned the oven to broil and not to bake."

"Not his fault," Mary continued, "but an experienced food preparer would have noticed my mistake early on and corrected it."

"So?" I again asked, not yet visualizing what was out of whack.

"So, the hens on the top pan are burned to a crisp, and the ones on the bottom pan are raw! That's the so!"

"Time to order out?" I asked, tensing my body in order to duck under the tongs she was waving in my direction.

"Nothing like a dinner party with takeout from McDonalds! They won't forget this evening—ever! You can kiss those potential clients goodbye!"

"How long will it take to cook the bottom rack?"

"Thirty minutes. But that won't work. The ones on top are burned!"

"Best thing to do," I said, stepping out of tong range, "is fess up."

"Best thing to do," my wife replied, "is for you to get back in there and eat your salad slowly. Very slowly. And keep them talking."

"For thirty minutes?"

"For two hours if necessary. Now go, while I try to fix this mess!"

So back into the dining room I went, took my seat, and quickly realized Mary's plan wasn't going to work. It made no difference how fast—or slow—I ate, the guests would eat at their own pace. Which, of course, they did.

There is a particular timing to dinner parties. Certainly not as critical as the timing of a football play or a rocket launch, but when dinner timing goes awry, a certain discomfort sets in. I didn't want to have that happen, so I worked at making conversation, worried that I wouldn't be able to distract our guests long enough. Murphy would soon be dancing a jig.

But Mary saved the day. A large glass of wine in her hand, she slipped into her seat, picked up her fork to begin eating her salad. She almost immediately put her fork down, looked around the room and said, "I have a confession to make." She then proceeded to explain that she had turned the oven to broil instead of bake, and, "well, the four hens in the bottom pan will be ready in a few more minutes, but the four on top are disasters. Two are burnt beyond repair, and two are marginal."

"I like mine well done. Crispy even," two of the guests volunteered. Whether that was true or not, it made the remainder of the evening work.

"David and I will try our hand at the charred ones. If you both don't mind extra crispy, then I think we can go on with the dinner. If not there's always take-out."

My memory is that our guests began telling their own stories of food disasters, and by the time dessert was served, the only disaster was the one in my wife's mind.

Final score: Tannenbaums 3, Murphy 0.

My Mother, The Clairvoyant

(Always Listen to Your Mommy)

It is commonplace for businesses to be bought and sold. Kraft buys Heinz. MCI buys Sprint. In some situations, there are multiple entities vying to buy a particular company, and a bidding war ensues. The process can often involve very tight time frames, since bids must be submitted on a schedule set by the seller.

In the scenario that follows, think entertainment company with worldwide operations as the company for sale, which we'll call BULLSEYE, and one of the potential buyers is someone named Adam Jones. Jones has studied BULLSEYE'S operations in great detail and has put together a management team of superior talent who can easily run BULLSEYE. The only kicker in Jones's plan is that he is millions short of what it will take to buy BULLSEYE.

Jones has approached a billionaire, Miss Moneybags, who I'll now refer to as MB, and convinced her that an investment by her will be pay high returns within five years. MB has run the numbers and from all indications has determined that the return should be better even than Jones has promised. This is a home run for all concerned.

With MB now enthusiastically backing him, Jones can continue the bidding process knowing he has the financial stamina to win. What had begun as ten potential buyers is now down to just two, Jones and one other suitor. The final sealed bid is due in the New York office of BULLSEYE's lawyer by noon on Wednesday, five days from now, including two weekend days.

My phone rings. It is one of my partners based in another city. That partner is representing MB, and it has been decided that she will contribute whatever it takes to win the bid, provided the intellectual property that BULLSEYE claims it owns is really owned by BULLSEYE and hasn't been sold or encumbered in any way. Remember that BULLSEYE is an entertainment company and its intellectual property, including its name, is perhaps its most valuable asset. Remember also that the intellectual property is spread around the world. I am given until Tuesday noon to provide assurances that the intellectual property is valid and unencumbered.

BULLSEYE's law firm has arranged to make all of the intellectual property files available in its office two blocks from mine but, alas, not until Sunday noon. "Okay," I say because there is nothing else I can say, even though we only have two days to get everything done. "We'll get on it."

Promptly at noon on Sunday, I, along with a young lawyer and two paralegals, am admitted to the law firm and essentially locked in a conference room piled high with boxes. By nine Monday morning, they (I had gone home around one in the morning to catch a few hours' sleep) had flagged a few problem areas and had at least one full legal pad of questions. BULLSEYE's law firm was busy providing answers, but there was no doubt this was going to take a day or two more because some of those answers had to come from time zones exactly opposite of ours.

At eleven on Monday, Adam Jones himself swept into the bullpen where we were working. Recall that MB was our firm's client, not Jones, but he had flown in to lend a hand, and our client had no objection to Jones being able to see for himself what the legal side of the intellectual property looked like. After all, it was he who would have to live with any mess we overlooked. Several more boxes arrived while we were briefing Jones, and I called for reinforcements. This was going to take another all-nighter, and perhaps even more.

"We're making progress, Mr. Jones," I said at about three in the afternoon, "but with these new files, we have hours of work ahead of us. That, and the fact that answers to our questions are not coming as quickly as we'd like from Japan and Brazil and several other places, means that it'll be at least morning until we know much more than we do now.

"I do have a problem, though," I continued. "Passover begins tonight, and I need to leave in a few minutes to be at the Seder. But I assure you my staff will continue on."

Jones took in what I had just told him, his eyes conveying deep concern. Then he capitulated. "So long as they can reach you if there's a problem."

"They know how to reach me," I responded, knowing my staff would only contact me during a Seder in a dire emergency and most likely not even then. And then I had a thought. "How would you like to join me at the Seder?"

"I'm not Jewish. I've never..."

"That's not an issue. I have a policy, started it in college, I always invite to my Seder anyone who is away from their own home on Passover. And you don't have to be Jewish."

"I don't know, if...Well, hell, yes. I've always wanted to see what a Seder is like, so I would be most honored to join you. But your wife? Won't she..."

"She's used to last-minute invitations on Passover. My parents will be there as well. I'll call to give my wife a heads up. And please don't bring anything but yourself."

Mary wasn't exactly happy, but what could she say? There was plenty of food and room at the table. And she had seen this last-minute Seder movie several times before.

At the Seder hour, the doorbell rang, and there Jones was, a dozen roses in his hand.

"I told you not..."

"You didn't cook the meal. This is for your wife. Women always enjoy flowers. Couldn't come empty-handed."

The Seder begins with a few prayers and quickly moves into the recounting of the story of the Israelites' exodus from Egypt. Dinner isn't served until the story telling is mostly over. Passover, being a celebration of freedom, is a good time for people to reflect on what freedom means to the world in general and to them in particular. That night, my daughter (of blessed memory) read an essay she had written on freedom. We ate, told stories, drank the traditional four glasses of wine (and perhaps more) and around ten thirty or eleven, Jones excused himself and said he had to get to his hotel for a call with Korea.

I walked him to the door and, thinking he had come by cab, offered to drive him to his hotel.

"No need," he said, "I have a driver out here in the driveway."

"Oh, my," I said, feeling horrible. "If I had known, he could have joined us. I feel..."

"Nonsense. I'll see you in the morning. I hope your team has good news. This is an important deal for me, and it's critical that your client be comfortable enough with the intellectual property to allow me to blow the other side away. I know what they're about to bid, and I plan to be a magnitude higher. Once your report is finished, it's in the bag."

A half hour later, I was helping in the kitchen when my eighty-year-old mother joined us. "I know it's none of my business," she began (as she often did when she was meddling in someone else's affairs), "but is that Jones guy a client of yours?"

"No mother, not a client." I couldn't tell her what Jones' business was, so I just said, "someone I know from work."

"Well...a word of advice. I know it's not my business, but something's not right with that man. He's a character if ever I met one."

"Mother, whatever are you talking about?"

"He's not an honest man, to put it bluntly. He lies."

"How would you possibly know such a thing? He's a respected businessman."

"Just the way he talks, the stories he tells. He's not honest. That's all I know. He's not an honest person."

"Mother, I sat across from you and I heard everything he said. I didn't hear anything dishonest." I quickly replayed the table conversation to be sure I hadn't missed anything. "I can't think of a thing he said that troubles me."

"He didn't say anything dishonest. He's just not an honest person, that's all. I probably shouldn't have said anything. It's not my business."

I couldn't think of anything to say, so I remained silent, still replaying the dinner conversation.

"Take it for what it's worth," my mother advised. "But if I were you, I'd not have him as a friend." She then marched out of the kitchen.

"Hope I didn't wake you," I said to my partner when he

answered the phone at five minutes to midnight, "but I have something to relate to you about Adam Jones."

"No, no. Been working. I just got off the phone with MB. She's approved the deal going forward, pending only your findings on the intellectual property. Your preliminary reports look fine. She's prepared to step up the financing to whatever level it takes to land the deal. The IP still okay?"

"The few wrinkles we found I believe we'll be able to put to bed by noon tomorrow," I said. "I don't anticipate any real problems. But that's not why I called." How do I say my mother thinks Jones is dishonest?

"Okay. Shoot."

Here goes. "Jones was at my house for Seder dinner tonight. My whole family was there. And...and I'm just going to tell you what happened, and you be the judge. My mother just came to me and for whatever reason, she believes he's not an honest person."

"What happened?"

"Nothing, really. Just normal dinner conversation. He told a few stories, nothing unusual. I certainly didn't pick anything up. But my mother says he's not an honest person."

"Do you trust your mother's judgment?"

"I suppose I wouldn't be on this call if I didn't. My mother does have very good instincts about people. But..."

"That's good enough for me. I'm passing this on to our client."

Note to Self: Self, this is lesson one in how to lose a client in one easy phone call. The old my mother made me do it routine. No basis whatsoever.

Twenty minutes later my partner was back on the phone. "MB says she trusts your mother's instinct. Tomorrow you are to slow roll the investigation. Give Jones nothing. We're hiring two investigative firms. One for the states and one internationally. Nothing goes forward until both reports are back."

"Got it."

"Oh, and MB thanks you for passing along your mother's instincts."

"What the hell's taking so long?" Jones barked when lunch was brought in the next day. "I thought we were close to wrapping this up. You told me we'd be done by mid-morning!"

"No answer back yet from Korea." That was correct as far as it went. But neither had we pressed them. "And I think that Brazil matter is more serious than it appeared at first."

"That's bull crap! I was down there when the incident happened and it's nothing. That lawsuit should have been settled months ago. There's no foundation for it. You're over-thinking it."

"As soon as we find record of a settlement we'll clear it," I said. "We're working on it as best we can."

"Your firm is incompetent if you think there's a problem. Get this cleared up—and do it fast!" He stormed from the room, not to be seen again that day. I believe his plan was to isolate our team and try to pry the money loose from our client without our report.

"David," my partner began, hours later, "keep the stall up. Don't give any indication that you're making progress."

"Why? What's up?"

"The first report came in from the stateside firm we hired. And it's not good. Nothing definitive, but they did pick up what they called some international rumblings. Don't yet know what to make of it, but MB's nervous."

"What the hell's holding up your report?" Jones bellowed in my ear at seven that night. I held the phone an arm's length from my ear and the sound level still hurt. "You're the only thing standing in the way of me becoming owner of BULL-SEYE. If I miss that bid because of you, your firm will pay big time!"

"I understand, but I can't..."

"I don't care what you understand! That bid is due in less than eighteen hours. It takes hours to process the guarantee bond, so I need an answer by midnight! You hear me?"

"I hear you. I'm doing my best," I said, doubting whether we'd hear anything in time for his deadline.

Note to Self: Don't answer the phone the next time it rings with his caller ID.

The international report was held up and the deadline passed without Jones making a bid. At least he didn't make a bid with MB's money behind him.

Two days later my phone did ring. It was my partner informing me that the international report had just been received. It seems that Adam Jones may have been involved in improprieties with two separate investors over the past five years. There was nothing conclusive either way, but MB was thankful to my mother for speaking up when she did.

I never did tell my mother what she had done. For that I will always be truly sorry.

THANK YOU

I again wish to thank my longtime friend Ron Slusky for his relentless suggestions, edits, advice, and commentary. He is a master at holding a mirror to my writing and forcing me to come to grips with the rough edges of which there are far more than I want to acknowledge. Ron occasionally grants me leeway with the storytelling, but he is a stickler for getting the law right, as he should be.

I also owe Kathlyn Auten and Meridith Murray special thanks for their valuable editing and advice.

And Kat Gally has once again rendered an amazing cover for which I am grateful. She is an exceptionally talented artist and a beautiful person.

Also, a big thank you to Harry Belafonte and Lord Burgess for giving us one of my all-time favorite songs. I have a fondness for the Caribbean because of that song.

Spouses hold a special place in our lives. Spouses of writers hold a particularly unique place in that they read early drafts and must deal with the age-old adage of "not telling the spouse he's ugly." Mary balances it all in a positive way, and her comments, insights, cautions, and encouragements are more than appreciated—I'd be lost without them—and without her. Thank you, beautiful woman, for being there for me each and every day.

ABOUT THE AUTHOR

David Harry Tannenbaum is a retired patent attorney who lives with his wife Mary and dog Franco in Pittsburgh, Pennsylvania, and Miromar Lakes, Florida.

David is the author of the award-winning *Out Of The Depths*, a story of survivor's guilt stemming from a doctor's teen years confined in a Nazi concentration camp; and *Standard Deviation*, centered around an Asperger's child and his interaction with three other troubled individuals. David is also the author, under the pen name David Harry, of six mystery/thrillers set on the porous Texas/Mexico border.

When he isn't writing, David enjoys model trains, biking, and traveling.

David can be reached at:

RedEnginePressInfo@gmail.com

authordavidtannenbaum@gmail.com

Facebook: DavidHarryTannenbaum

Twitter: DHTannenbaum

BOOKS BY

David Harry Tannenbaum

Standard Deviation

Out Of The Depths

David Harry

The Padre Puzzle

The Padre Predator

The Padre Paranoia

The Padre Pandemic

The Padre Poison

The Padre Phantom

Soon to be Released

The Padre Phony